MESOAMERICAN RELIGIONS AND ARCHAEOLOGY

ESSAYS IN PRE-COLUMBIAN CIVILIZATIONS

Aleksandar Bošković

ARCHAEOPRESS PRE-COLUMBIAN ARCHAEOLOGY 7

ARCHAEOPRESS PUBLISHING LTD
GORDON HOUSE
276 BANBURY ROAD
OXFORD OX2 7ED

www.archaeopress.com

ISBN 978 1 78491 502 5
ISBN 978 1 78491 503 2 (e-Pdf)

Cover: Tikal, Structure 5D-43, probably built before 700 CE, with the Temple of the Jaguar (Temple I) in the background. The structure was built along the East Plaza Ballcourt, and it is one of the finest examples of the "talud-tablero" style, which was typical of Teotihuacan in Central Mexico, and probably exported to Tikal with the new ruling family in the late 4th century CE.
Back cover: Ceramic vessel with the duck-shaped lid. Petexbatún, Guatemala, around 700 CE.

Printed in England by Oxuniprint, Oxford

This book is available direct from Archaeopress or from our website www.archaeopress.com

Contents

List of Figures

Foreword

Modernity involves increasing specialization and the extraction of knowledge from its context; Bruno Latour argues that we have never been modern, even if academic disciplines tend in that direction. For the hard sciences, hyper-specialization has produced impressive advances. For the social sciences and interpretative fields, it often results in models and conventions that become ever more removed from the reality they seek to describe.

Like hemlines and haircuts, theoretical approaches ebb and flow in cycles. Is it structure that produces subjectivity or is it human agency that builds structures? Does history produce the present or is our view of history but a rearward projection of current concerns? The human sciences, despite the complexity of the subject matter, keep coming back to a very few basic questions.

In this collection of insightful essays, Aleksandar Bošković grapples with the big questions of the human condition as grounded in the particular circumstances and histories of Mesoamerican cultures. He rejects the sterility of abstract theory while calling on its insights, artfully grapping with existential issues in the context of native American linguistics and religious particulars. Bošković builds on a rich tradition in Mesoamerican studies of polymaths weaving together methods, contexts, and histories in narrative accounts unbound by narrow disciplinary conventions.

In fact, Bošković takes his epistemological inspiration from the ancient Maya themselves, who were decidedly not modern, at least to the extent that Latourian purification defines modernity. A hallmark of Classic Maya cosmologies is their integration: science and religion, governance and economy, astronomy and architecture—all were part and parcel of one system. And imbalance in one area could produce ill results in another. Crop growth was tied to religious ritual, which was linked to astronomy, and so on. The universe was seen as intensely and intimately interconnected, in a way that we in contemporary academia might call interdisciplinary or multidimensional. At the same time, as Bošković makes clear, this was not a monolithic system; for example, the (singular) pantheon of gods we attribute to the Maya was actually composed of locally variable and heterogeneous sets of deities.

In this collection Bošković combines review and critique with original contributions. The style is effective—we get an overview of major works in the field since the 1980s as well as a deep dive into a number of areas. Focusing on pre-Columbian civilizations, Bošković's approach is more than nominally archaeological, but this is archaeology in context: not just artifacts, but also the art and iconography, the extant oral traditions and ethno-historical literature. He includes the often overlooked tradition in Serbo-Croatian and Slovenian – and the surprising role Vinko Paletin played in the conquest of Yucatan (and his unfortunate defense of war against the Indians). There is also an enlightening exegesis of the Codex Borbonicus.

The result is a holistic approach to understanding pre-Columbian civilization. I first met Aleksandar Bošković in New Orleans in the early 1990s when we were both attending Tulane for graduate school in anthropology. Professor Munro Edmunson led our obligatory graduate seminar on the history of anthropological theory, and he was everything I imagined a brilliant professor to be—erudite, of course, and a quick wit, he commanded an amazing expanse of material, from philosophy to psychology to astronomy and anthropology. He inevitably quoted in the original, whatever that may have been for a particular topic, and most likely had an opinion about the etymology of a difficult word. Bošković once gave him a copy of a book he had written in Serbo-Croatian, and Ed (as we all called him) glanced through it and pointed to a typo.

Bošković carries on the grand tradition of Munro Edmunson and such exceptional scholars not content to stay inside narrow disciplinary boxes or to reproduce conventional wisdom. Rather Bošković is driven to understand the Maya and the Olmecs and the other Mesoamerican civilizations on their own terms and in their own context. The result is this wonderful collection of essays that students of Mesoamerican studies will value for years to come.

Edward F Fischer (Vanderbilt University)
30 December 2016

Acknowledgements

My journey into Pre-Columbian Mesoamerica was very much influenced by "chance and serendipity" – to use the expression I heard from my colleague from Sweden, Professor Ulf Hannerz, some years ago at Durham. Over the years, I was very fortunate to have the support of some brilliant people and formidable scholars. They shared their insights and knowledge, provided important suggestions, invited me to lectures and meetings (like Baudez did at Sorbonne, whenever I was in Paris), and were always ready to comment on my papers. In retrospect, meeting some of them almost looks accidental, but they have certainly left their mark, and I am humbled to have had the opportunity to meet them, to learn from them, and to discuss aspects of interpretation (especially when it comes to methodology) with them. My interest in first Maya, and later Mesoamerican studies, was sparked by the writings of the late Mr Tibor Székely (1912-1988), citizen of the world in a true meaning of this word, and one of the world's leading Esperanto scholars. I was fortunate to meet him at his home in Subotica, in the Vojvodina province, in 1987, and I was also quite lucky that he was able to contribute a number of entries in the *Dictionary of Non-Classical Mythology*, a project that I co-edited, and for which I wrote over 150 entries (Bošković, Vukomanović and Jovanović 2015).

The interest in ancient Maya brought me to Tulane University in 1990. I was supervised by Professor Munro S. Edmonson (1924-2002), a man of fascinating erudition and vast knowledge, who was also an amazing scholar, and a great believer in humanity ("human nature"). Edmonson was instrumental in my "discovery" of important ethnohistorical sources related to the ancient Maya. I was also very fortunate to be introduced into the ancient Mexican art (and interpretation of Mexican manuscript paintings in particular) by another great scholar, Professor Mary Elizabeth Smith (1932-2004). While at Tulane, my research in Guatemala was supported by the Matilda Geddings Gray Fellowship, as well as by the help by the Instituto de Antropología e Historia de Guatemala (IDAEH). Over the years, I also benefited from the critical conversations and support by Professor Richard E. W. Adams (1931-2015) from the University of Texas at San Antonio, and Dr. Claude-François Baudez (1932-2013) from the CNRS in Paris. Another colleague from Paris, Dr. Bertrand Masquelier (also from CNRS) helped me to get the access to the original manuscript of the *Codex Borbonicus*, at the *Bibliothèque de l'Assemblée Nationale*, in 1992.

In Belgrade, I owe immense gratitude to my friend Ms Miroslava Malešević from the Ethnographic Institute of the Serbian Academy of Sciences and Arts, who introduced me to Evon Z. Vogt (1918-2004) during his 1989 visit. Professor Vogt was also very helpful for the early stages of my research – as well as in providing contextual information on the reception of my paper on Maya myths. As one of the first academic texts that I wrote was published in the *Bulletin of the Ethnographic Institute of the Serbian Academy of Sciences and Arts* (actually a commentary on the chapter from Edmonson's edition of the *Chilam Balam of Chumayel* – Bošković 1988b; Edmonson 1986), I also acknowledge the support of the Secretary of the Academy and one of the most prominent world Neolithic archaeologists, Dragoslav Srejović (1931-1996). Professor Srejović was passionate about symbolism and religion in archaeological context, and he saw the value of publishing something on a topic both geographically and culturally distant from Serbia as very important for the local scientific community.

My friend William H. Fisher from the College of William & Mary helped me with some language issues (especially with the parts of the text originally written in Serbo-Croatian), but also provided a crucial critical reading of the whole manuscript. Dr. Sanja Brekalo Pelin sent me a book from Madrid, Mr Slavoljub Bajčetić helped with several illustrations used in this book, and another friend from Belgrade, Mr Nemanja Milićević, was most helpful in setting the text together. Last but not least, the publisher of this book, Archaeopress, proved to be very supportive, and I especially acknowledge the timely and precise communication and guidance I received from Dr. David Davison.

There is something to be said about the phrase "standing on the shoulders of Giants" (as famously put by Bernard Sylvester of Chartres around 12th century CE) – many times I felt that I could arrive at some important insights only because some great people have laid the foundations for it in the past, and I was fortunate enough to meet them and discuss with them. I could also conclude with a quote from another person who was very helpful in my work since 1990, Clifford Geertz (1926-2006), when he observed that: "The essential vocation of interpretive anthropology is not to answer our deepest questions, but to make available to us answers that others, guarding other sheep in other valleys, have given, and thus to include them in the consultable record of what man has said" (1973: 30). Over the years, a number of friends and colleagues from different places, like Henyo Trinidade Barretto Filho, Erik Bähre, Thomas Hylland Eriksen, Edward F. Fischer, Miroslava Malešević, Antonádia Monteiro Borges, Isak Niehaus, Mariza Peirano, Maja Petrović Šteger, Nigel Rapport and Milan Vukomanović turned out to be important, occasionally critical, but always extremely valuable interlocutors, making available to me important "answers that others, guarding other sheep in other valleys, have given." Their presence contributed to my studies and made me a better person. Of course, none of the people mentioned here bears any responsibility for any potential omissions or errors.

Preface

This book contains book reviews, review essays and articles dealing with different aspects of Pre-Columbian civilizations of ancient America, most of them published between 1989 and 2014 in *Anthropos*, but also in *American Antiquity, Bulletin of the Ethnographic Institute of the Serbian Academy of Sciences & Arts (SASA), Bulletin of the Slovene Ethnological Society, Human Mosaic*, and *Indiana*. The chapter on Codex Cihuacoatl (or Codex Borbonicus, chapter 8) was originally written in 1992 for the Seminar in Mexican Manuscript Painting at Tulane University (with Mary Elizabeth Smith), revised in 1993, and later published (in again revised form) in the Serbo-Croatian translation (Bošković 2006). When it was originally published in mid-1989, "The Meaning of Maya Myths" was the first article on this subject in English – studies by Taube (1992, 1993) and Miller and Taube (1993) followed later. In the meantime, some of the books that I wrote about have gone through multiple editions (Ch. 2), and some have served as important markers in our understanding of these cultures (Ch. 1). Some have also demonstrated the limitations of using incomplete data (Ch. 11), but others have become classics in their field (Ch. 18). All of the texts were slightly revised and updated. What ties all of these texts together is insistence on clear *methodology*, supported by the *field research*. This methodology is inseparable from the *context* of specific archaeological finds, and it helps us put these cultures and societies in a *historical* perspective. The choice of the books and topics reflects my own geographical/regional interests, which included Guatemala and Central Mexico – so, unfortunately, there is not enough on South American cultures. This, however, is simply a consequence of personal experience, nothing more. On the other hand, I believe that the basic methodological principles set forth in this book (as well as the moral stance advocated by archaeologists referred to here) have relevance for the study of all Pre-Columbian civilizations of the Americas.

When it comes to *method*, I agree with the approach taken by Adams, Sabloff, Sharer and other notable archaeologists about the importance of what Richard E. W. Adams has called "field archaeology school" approach (Adams 1989, personal communication). As he put it: "Excavated data are quite important, but we also consider epigraphy, iconography, ethnology, and native literatures" (ibid.). Several decades ago, art historian George Kubler also pointed to the importance of combining different disciplines in order to interpret ancient Amerindian cultures (1990: 32-34). The alternative approach, focusing on art history and art criticism, puts an emphasis on artefacts (especially ceramics) that have no provenience. This raises the problems of authenticity, along with different legal and moral problems, but also the loss of *context* – leading to loss of information. This is very obvious for anyone who has conducted archaeological research, and had to deal with the destruction left by looters. Again, as put by Adams:

> An example of this loss of information is that of the Altar Vase and the 40 printed pages of description and interpretation that were possible because it was found in excavation. It is clearly a scene of an historical event, a funeral of the female ruler of Altar de Sacrificios (1989, personal communication; cf. also Adams 1971).

Furthermore, as authentication and evaluation of unprovenienced ceramics were used for items stolen from Belize, Guatemala, Honduras, Mexico and Peru (to list only some countries that have had to deal with this problem) – as these items could not be exported legally from their countries of origin, Adams also noted that:

> Authentication and evaluation is against the code of ethics of the Society for American Archaeology because it adds to commercial exploitation of the cultural patrimony of various victim countries. Therefore there is a real tension between field archaeologists who abide by the rules and those who do not (1989, personal communication).

The moral issue of whether to use or not to use artefacts (especially painted polychrome ceramics) from the looted tombs and of unknown provenience has been with archaeologists, anthropologists, and art historians for decades. Some influential anthropologists, like Michael D. Coe, have enthusiastically approved their use: "My feeling was then, and still is, that all of these materials, even though looted (like the majority of Greek pots or Chinese bronzes) ought to be put out in the public domain so that scholars could study them" (2000: 209). On the other hand, one of the most distinguished archaeologists and epigraphers (and someone who has had personal experiences with looters, who killed a member of his team in Guatemala), Ian Graham, saw things differently:

> To begin with, the pieces most in demand among institutional and wealthier private collectors were stone sculptures, for they proclaimed status more emphatically than ceramics. The damage to archaeology caused by this trade [in stolen objects – A. B.] often embraced not only loss of provenance, but of part of the hieroglyphic inscriptions too, since those on the back or sides of a stela were often cut off to lighten it for clandestine removal. (2002: 909)

In their article for the *Annual Review of Anthropology* written over a decade ago, Brodie and Renfrew quoted from the Archaeological Institute of America Code of Ethics, which stipulates that

> [Members should] refuse to participate in the trade of undocumented antiquities and refrain from activities that enhance the commercial value of such objects. Undocumented antiquities are those which are not documented as belonging to a public or private collection before December 30, 1970 (...) or which have not been excavated and exported from the country of origin in accordance with the laws of that country. (Brodie and Renfrew 2005: 352)

Furthermore, the International Council of Museums noted in its own Code of Ethics that "Museums should not acquire objects where there is reasonable cause to believe that their recovery involved the unauthorized, unscientific, or intentional destruction or damage of monuments, archaeological or geological sites" (Brodie and Renfrew 2005: 351).

In the review of an earlier Renfrew's book (Renfrew 2002), and while understanding the excitement of some epigraphers and their desire to have *all* the objects that could help them understand scenes from painted ceramics that might refer to religion or myths, Graham wrote that it would have been wiser to wait a little bit and use the numerous sources found and documented during actual archaeological excavations instead of spectacular but unprovenienced materials. Given archaeologists' reluctance to take into account unprovenienced objects, it is no surprise that M. D. Coe's remarkable and elegantly written summary of the history of the decipherment of Maya script ends in bitter disappointment over archaeologists' apparent lack of understanding of the importance of these new discoveries (2000: 255 ff). Perhaps the fact that, by 1983, almost sixty per cent of all the Maya sites in Belize have been damaged by looters (Brodie and Renfrew 2005: 346) has something to do with it?

FIG. 1. STELA 4, UCANAL, GUATEMALA, 849. HEIGHT: 1.9M. MUSEO NACIONAL DE ANTROPOLOGÍA E HISTORIA DE GUATEMALA.

I believe that archaeological and anthropological research is in itself exciting enough to not need stolen artefacts, forged vases, fantastic stories and invented mythical genealogies or, as Adams put it in his letter, "scholarship founded on sand." There are numerous examples that clearly demonstrate how the use of the archaeological research (and the data acquired *in context* – as pointed by Ian Graham and Richard Adams) provided fascinating and very detailed information about ancient sites – like, for example, Tikal (Coe 1965, 1988, 1990; Sabloff 2003), or much smaller Altar de Sacrificios (Adams 1971) or Río Azul (Adams 1986, 1987, 1999), all in today's Guatemala. In writing this book, my main intent was to produce both a methodologically sound and ethically valid interdisciplinary introduction into this exciting world, as well as an overview of the different topics (mostly dealing with culture and religion) that remain important in the study of Pre-Columbian civilizations.

Part One – Cultures in Context

1. Regional Perspectives on the Olmec

Robert J. Sharer, and David C. Grove (eds.), *Regional Perspectives on the Olmec*. Cambridge: Cambridge University Press, 1989. xxxvi +386 pp. (SAR Advanced Seminar Series)

This impressive volume presents studies by ten leading North American anthropologists about the complex of cultures that used to be considered Mesoamerica's first civilization (Soustelle 1979a). Eight of the contributors participated in the School for Advanced Research seminar that took place in Santa Fe, New Mexico in 1983, and this seminar in effect presented the whole history of "Olmec studies." The book also includes a contribution by Michael D. Coe, who still believes that the Olmecs from the Gulf of Mexico between 1500 and 500 BCE laid foundations for all the later civilizations in this part of the world – a similar opinion was expressed in chapters written by Gareth Lowe and Tom Lee. On the other hand, according to other participants of the seminar, the word "Olmec" and the adjectives derived from it should be used with much more caution, as archaeological data point to the fact that several other cultures across Mesoamerica develop at approximately the same time – and the one from the Gulf of Mexico is just one of them. As a matter of fact, the word "Olmec" is derived from the Náhuatl expression *olmeca, uixtotin*, which can be freely translated as "people from the land of the rubber tree, the ones who live on the edge of the salt water" – the term used by 16th century inhabitants of Central Mexico to refer to the people from the Gulf of Mexico. It requires a really wild stretch of imagination to assume that these people had anything in common with the people who lived in the same area more than 2,500 years earlier (Bošković 1989).

In her contribution, Joyce Marcus presented a perspective from the Valley of Oaxaca, while Grove and Sharer presented results of their research in Chalcatzingo (Mexico) and Chalchuapa (Salvador) respectively. From an archaeological perspective, a decisive blow to the theory about the omnipresence of Olmecs is presented by Paul Tolstoy who argues that the alleged "Olmec" funerary figurines found at several sites in Central Mexico actually represent an autochthonous art style as well as that they are not present in the core area from which the "Olmec civilization" is supposed to have emerged from.

One of the goals of this School for Advanced Research seminar was to show whether there was anything like a "civilization" in this area 3,000 years ago. Although there was no consensus about this issue (nor was it expected), the prevailing opinion was that the Olmec social organization was at an intermediary stage between a tribal community with strict hierarchy (*chiefdom*) and a "proper" state. Grove's suggestion from the Introduction is that an alternative term should replace the word "Olmec," and he proposed a value-neutral term "complex X." Although this suggestion did not receive the support, one of the direct consequences of this important meeting and the book is that all the terms related to "Olmecs" are used in scholarly research with much more caution in scholarly research. It is also important to stress the importance of this book for some later (and much more general) works about the topic (Magni 2003), as well as the history of research about the ancient cultures of the Gulf of Mexico (Grove 2014).

This volume clearly demonstrated all the advantages of using a *regional approach* in Mesoamerican studies. In the aftermath of its publication this approach became accepted practice in all publications dealing with ancient Pre-Columbian civilizations. Since a universalist approach (according to which everything was interpreted from the perspective of a single culture and a unique cultural heritage) could not provide answers to the questions that anthropologists and archaeologists asked, it turned out that studying each site (or a complex of sites) individually from an intrinsic perspective (taking into account of all the external influences and contacts) aids better understanding of Mesoamerican civilizations. That is why perhaps the greatest importance of this book is that it catalyzed a change of methodology (or a shift in dominant paradigm as Thomas Kuhn would put it), and a first step towards better understanding of a fascinating world.

2. Comparing Changes in Mesoamerica

Richard E. Blanton, Stephen A. Kowalewski, Gary M. Feinman, and Laura M. Finstein, *Ancient Mesoamerica. A Comparison of Change in Three Regions.* 2nd edition. Cambridge: Cambridge University Press, 1993. 284 pp. (New Studies in Archaeology)

This book was first published in 1981, with Blanton, Kowalewski, and Feinman as authors. The new, revised edition with Finsten added to the list of contributors, follows the pattern of revising the major general works on Mesoamerica in order to incorporate the most recent developments in this area (for example, R. E. W. Adams' *Prehistoric Mesoamerica* has been reissued several times; the same goes for regional studies like the ones about the Maya by Sharer and Demarest). A notable addition to this edition is a bibliographic essay (226-242) in which the authors briefly discuss different works related to the study of ancient Mesoamerican cultures.

The title "Ancient Mesoamerica" might be a misnomer, since the book actually examines processes of change and adaptation in only three regions: the Valley of Oaxaca, the Valley of Mexico, and the eastern lowlands. In terms of major cultures, special emphasis is on the Mixtec and Zapotec (Valley of Oaxaca), the Teotihuacan, Toltec, and Aztec (Valley of Mexico), and the lowland Maya (eastern lowlands). Despite the expertise that the authors display in dealing with such a diverse topic, one might also point out that their main professional interests (particularly associated with the long-term field projects) are connected with the Valley of Oaxaca, and their first hand experience of other areas is somewhat limited. Nevertheless, they present an excellent comparative survey of the regions they discuss, with frequent comparisons with ethnographical, archaeological, and theoretical data coming from other areas of the world. This certainly helps to put Mesoamerican civilizations in a more global perspective, and to stop regarding them only as exotic exceptions from everything known from the "classical" Western heritage.

Although the book has been advertised as the one that assumes "no prior knowledge of Mesoamerican archaeology or cultural evolution," some background is extremely helpful for understanding the contributors' theoretical claims. The main argument of the book is connected with the theoretical and practical implications of "cultural evolution," so it is obvious that someone who rejects the basic premises of this theory will reject the theoretical arguments of the book. Blanton, Kowalewski, Feinman, and Finsten define their goal as offering "a current assessment of the nature and causes of cultural evolution in Mesoamerica" (27). The term "evolution" here does not signify a series of progressive stages; the authors are primarily interested in change in human societies, with the main factors of interest being scale, integration, complexity, and boundedness. Of course, the selection of these four features rather than others that may influence culture change is arbitrary to some extent, but it is in accord with the contributors' intention to "use a type of systems approach designed to schematize flows of goods or information or people among actual groups that existed in space, such as households or administrative districts" (13).

The book is divided in six chapters: "The growth of Mesoamerican archaeology and ethnohistory," "Preceramic Mesoamerica" (both of which include examples outside the Valleys of Oaxaca and Mexico or the eastern lowlands), "The Valley of Oaxaca," "The Valley of Mexico," "The eastern lowlands," and "Comparisons and conclusions." Because of the difficulties associated with the terrain and the vegetation, the eastern lowlands were not surveyed as well as the highland regions of Mexico, so the controlled comparison that the authors employ is somewhat vague in this respect. It is unclear whether the authors believe that the "Classic Maya collapse" actually occurred in the late 9th and early 10th century CE (187-190), since they do mention examples of Lamanai in Belize and the Puuc sites in the north-western Yucatan, where there is no sign of "collapse." In fact, in most sites within the territory of Belize, the "Classic Maya collapse" simply never happened, or happened in different time periods. For example Cerros "collapsed" around 3rd century CE and a similar thing at a similar time happened to the great Petén centres of Nakbé and El Mirador.[1]

Overall, this is a very readable and detailed account of the change and adaptation in three well studied and comparatively well documented regions of Mesoamerica. The particular strength of this volume is the insistence on combined approaches that take into account not only micro- and interregional, but also macro regional change and variation. Of course, given the pace of the research in Mesoamerican archaeology, they might be tempted to revise this volume again in a few years' time.

---

[1]   On a more general level, archaeologists like Demarest claim "there is still disagreement as to the nature and causes of the end of the lowland Classic Maya kingdoms" (2013: 22). See also Izquierdo-Egea (2015).

3. Pre-Columbian Ceramics and the Maya

Emma Sánchez Montañes, *La ceramic precolombina: el barro que los indios hicieron arte*. 128 pp., illustrations. Madrid: Anaya, 1988. (Biblioteca Iberoamericana, 6)
Andrés Ciudad, *Los mayas: el pueblo de los sacerdotes sabios*. 128 pp., illustrations. Madrid: Anaya, 1988. (Biblioteca Iberoamericana, 8)

As the world approached 1992 and the 500-year anniversary of what would from an Eurocentric perspective be called "the discovery of the New World" and from a more moderate one "the encounter of the two worlds," but also "the perspective of the conquered ones" (Léon-Portilla 1959) – a number of meetings and symposia were organized and hundreds of books published, with the general aim of somehow bringing the two worlds together. The problem lies in the multifacetedness of the two worlds. There are multiple contrasting (and, more often than not, conflicting) dichotomies: on the one side, Europeans, on the other, Indians (or Native Americans), then on the one side descendants of Europeans – and on the other people of mixed races, like Brazilian *mulattos*, on the one hand, the rich – on the other, the poor, Christians on the one side – adherents of traditional religions and customs on the other, educated ones on one side – uneducated ones on the other, etc. It is clear that many social groups from these dichotomies overlap, and that many occasionally "cross" from one "world" into another, and from one side of the dichotomy into its (supposed) opposite, which further complicates attempts to interpret interactions. At the same time, this renders more difficult the comprehension of the relationship between the interpreters and the ones who are being interpreted (Geertz 1988: 3-5). Under these circumstances, one of the possibilities is to follow what Max Weber (1946: 140) proposed as a "value-neutral" perspective, or to attempt to interpret events and cultural horizons within the context in which they originated, taking into account the existing historical and cultural factors, and avoiding mixing up attitudes that are product of our (contemporary) culture, with the ones of (ancient) cultures, that we try to interpret and study. Following up on this, a wealth of ethnographic data from Mesoamerica offers possibilities for different interpretations, but also for unjustified and unjustifiable "copy-pasting" of contemporary beliefs and rituals into distant past, with complete neglect of the cultural evolution and adjustments to the changed spiritual, social, economic and ecological circumstances. This was characteristic of the method of "ethnographic analogy" and quite present in Mesoamerican studies – despite the fact that some prominent scholars have long ago warned about the traps associated with this approach (Vogt 1964). Unfortunately, drawing "ethnological analogies" is quite present in other areas as well, and it is the last resort for the scholars who lack evidence to support their claims. I do not think that the value of the "proofs" based on analogies that "jump over" whole millennia, and operate with concepts as vague as "general unity of human mind" (which is supposed to operate in exactly the same way everywhere, regardless of the specific circumstances), needs to be discussed in more detail.

One of the interesting ways of interpretation was present in the newly established series of the Spanish publisher Anaya, with the idea that well-qualified scholars write for the general audience about different aspects of Latin American cultures. The books are all small size, hardcover, 128 pages each, with many colour illustrations, and with the outstanding quality of print. Thus, they present readers with clear text, which is at the same time visually and aesthetically pleasing.

Emma Sánchez Montañes'[2] text is an excellent introduction to the study of ancient Pre-Columbian ceramics. Following upon introductory remarks on ceramics as a testimony of the long vanished cultures, specific techniques of production (as is well known, even the pottery wheel was not used in ancient America – although toys with wheels were made), multiple functions of ceramics, and relationship between ceramics and culture, the first chapter of the book ends with considerations of the controversial origins of South American ceramics. During 1960s, some researchers assumed that Valdivia ceramics from present-day Ecuador (approximately 3500-1800 BCE) was "imported" or its manufacturing technique "brought" from the Jomon, on the present-day Japanese island Kyushu (the style that is credited as "the oldest pottery in Japan"). This hypothesis was immediately picked up by prominent diffusionists, like Betty J. Meggers (1965). As modern humans did not originate in the Americas, Meggers and her colleagues concluded that Amerindian cultures should not be considered as autochthonous, and it took some effort to establish the whole sequence of ceramics found on the coast of Ecuador. In the meantime, it was established that the ceramics in Ecuador actually *predates* the one found in Japan – and that was the end of the diffusionists' argument. The second chapter of the book deals with Mesoamerican ceramics, with special emphasis on very complex figurines found on the Pacific coast of Mexico, and their importance for understanding daily life (as many scenes, even depicting events from households, were depicted very realistically), then there are also "laughing heads" from the Gulf of Mexico, funerary urns from Oaxaca, Maya funerary ceramics, and several examples of true masterpieces from the island of Jaina, necropolis of Mayan aristocrats by the northeast coast of the Yucatán peninsula. I believe that this chapter could have been even better – had she made references to a catalogue of Maya painted vases found in archaeological context (Foncerrada de Molina y Lombardo de Ruiz 1979).

In the third chapter, Sánchez Montañes presents an overview of the ceramics from the Caribbean, Columbia, Venezuela, and Ecuador (unfortunately, probably due to the lack of space, no mention of some extremely interesting examples from Costa Rica), while the fourth part is dedicated to the ancient Peruvian ceramics. This is the longest, most detailed, and probably the best part of this overview, probably because of the focus on a spatially relatively limited area. The author focused on the funerary symbolism of different objects and Moche ceramics (150-800 CE – Holmquist Pachas y Bellina de los Heros 2010), with examples of some of the most beautiful ceramic objects ever created in the Americas (Quigler 2002). Of course, there is also the unavoidable chapter on the erotic symbolism of Moche figurines, as they present a unique case of the importance of sexual act in plastic arts, depicted with great realism and the emphasis on details. The

---

[2] Professor in the Anthropology of the Americas Department, University of Madrid.

final, fifth part of the book, presents an overview of Amazonia, north Argentina, ancient Amerindian cultures of the present-day USA, as well as maintenance of the production techniques in contemporary communities, and the transformation of ceramics under the influence of Christianity.

Given the scope of the area that Sánchez Montañes had to cover in her book, it would seem that Andres Ciudad Ruiz[3] had a much easier task. However, his work was the very first general overview of Maya civilization written in Spanish – and this was quite a burden. It sounds paradoxical, but there were many chronicles and accounts of the aspects of Maya culture published in Spanish, there were translations of books originally written in English (like Coe 2011), but no general account about the civilization that was the object of Spanish conquest that lasted until the end of the 17th century (Jones 1998).

Ciudad proceeded in a systematic way, using the most recent archaeological data that he had at the time. His book is divided in six chapters. The one entitled "Environment and Man" [sic] deals with the specifics of the geographic area, population and language, while the next chapter presents a brief historical overview. The third chapter is especially interesting, with general remarks about economy, trade, social stratification, and political structure. The next chapter deals with art and architecture, while the fifth one focuses on scientific achievements – especially arithmetic, calendar, and astronomy – and writing. The final chapter presents some general considerations about religion. Unfortunately, in this chapter, Ciudad diverts from the "value-neutral" approach, and describes religion almost like an instrument of control of the masses, devised by the ruling elites.[4] Occasionally one almost gets an impression that Ciudad sees religion as something similar to (or the remnant of) the "primitive mentality" – a view that could easily slip into evolutionism. It is a pity that he did not consider this aspect of ancient Maya life with the same passion and involvement as when he described economic relations, but it seems that he was much closer to material-determinism, which tends to underestimate the importance of ideological (as well as spiritual, non-material) aspects of life.

With all their good sides and bad sides, pros and cons, both books described here attempt to offer interpretation of their subjects from an *emic* perspective – from the structure and interconnectedness of their internal elements. Of course, there are some prejudices (like Ciudad's apparent dislike for religion, noted above), but it is important that the general audience is presented with the wealth of data and reliable information, both as an overview of past civilizations, and as a description of some contemporary processes (the place of ceramics in contemporary world; the role of the Maya traditional cultures today). The fact that Ciudad's book is still (in 2016) the only general text of its kind in Spanish, written by a Spanish scholar, also speaks about the relevance and importance of the texts published by the Editorial Anaya almost three decades ago.

---

[3] Also Professor in the Anthropology of the Americas Department, University of Madrid. Former President of the Sociedad Española de Estudios Mayas (SEEM).
[4] This type of prejudice is absent from general accounts of ancient Maya culture published in German (Riese 2011), French (Taladoire 2003; Baudez 2004; Baudez et Picasso 1987), or Serbo-Croatian (Bošković 1990, 2006).

FIG. 2. MAYA CERAMIC VESSEL FROM PETEXBATÚN AREA, LATE CLASSIC (600-700 CE).

4. Explaining Copan

E. Wyllys Andrews and William L. Fash (eds.), *Copan: The History of an Ancient Maya Kingdom*. Santa Fe: School of American Research Press; Oxford: James Currey, 2005. 492 pp.

This book comes out of the School of American Research (SAR) Advanced Seminar held in Santa Fe, New Mexico, in October 1994. It is also one of the final chapters in the long history of research at this site in present-day Honduras that has been a focal point of interest since 1576. Copan reached its major importance during the "Classic" period of ancient Maya civilization, and between 426 and 822 CE it was ruled by a single dynasty. The exploits of the "kingdom's" rulers and the fortunes of the "city's" inhabitants are well documented both in hieroglyphic texts (epigraphy) and in architecture. Here I put both terms in quotation marks, as they are a bit questionable in a more general historical and cultural context, despite many Maya archaeologists' preference for "kingdom," for example. Copan was neither the biggest nor the most important ancient Maya site, but due to the extraordinary amount of attention it has received, it is one of the best studied and also one where different theories and hypotheses could be tested.

The book consists of a Preface and eleven chapters written by fifteen scholars. Five of them were heading various parts of the Copan Acropolis Archaeological Project, which ended in 1994. These chapters add an important level of expertise. They all deal with different themes – ranging from the more general ones like social history, life of the elites, and political ecology, to the particular studies of specific structures and residences. Mesoamericanists, as well as students of prehistoric societies, will find very interesting overviews dealing with "contributions and controversies" (by William L. Fash and Ricardo Agurcia Fasquelle), as well as the one on "Issues in Copan Archaeology" (by E. Wyllys Andrews and William L. Fash). Finally, one of the premier Maya epigraphers, David Stuart, contributed another gem in his article on writing and representation of history on an ancestral shrine.

The contributions of this volume add to our understanding of this magnificent site, although they underemphasize the more general context of Copan's history. For example, we know that it was greatly influenced by the neighbouring Quirigua – but what about other sites (or "kingdoms"), like Tikal? It is now well established that there were frequent shifts in power and alliances between members of Classic Maya elites, and the roles played by smaller "kingdoms" should be considered. Also, the earlier volume in the SAR series on Tikal (Sabloff 2003), seems to be much more in tune with the attempts to understand a general Maya (and Mesoamerican) cultural history. Among the examples of relatively recent volumes dedicated to other major sites, one could also mention the one on Calakmul, published in Mexico (Vidal Angles and Domínguez Turriza 2003). The level of *local knowledge* produced in the Copan volume is truly amazing – but how does it fit into the history of the ancient Maya, especially following major advances in epigraphy and our understanding of various social and cultural processes that occurred over the last decade? Another peculiarity of this book is that it was published almost full eleven years after the SAR Advanced Seminar. This is highly unusual – for example, the already mentioned Tikal volume in the same series was published in early 2003 (and the Advanced Seminar dedicated to it held in 1999) – and maybe there is another interesting story to be uncovered in another chapter, yet to be written. Or perhaps in another book.

5. Vision and Revision

Flora S. Clancy and Peter D. Harrison (eds.), *Vision and Revision in Maya Studies*. Albuquerque: University of New Mexico Press, 1991. x + 224 pp., figures, maps, notes, index, bibliography.

The question of revisionism in archaeology is connected with the ever-present need to expand our understanding – especially concerning prehistoric cultures. It is sometimes associated with the postmodern approach in philosophy and history (as the editors of this volume note in the Introduction [p. xii]), but also can be related to post-processual methodology. In the context of Maya studies, this would mean trying to let the ancient (and modern, where possible) Maya speak for themselves, and trying to limit the work of interpretation as much as possible, eventually shifting to a hermeneutical approach.

Vision and Revision in Maya Studies consists of twelve papers presented at a conference at the University of New Mexico in Albuquerque in January 1987, framed by the editors' theoretical Introduction. According to the editors, "The title Vision & Revision in Maya Studies is meant to prepare the reader for what is to follow by reflecting the present state of Maya Studies" (p. vii). And indeed, some of the contributions are very much revisionist, aiming at completely new models that emerge from more recent ceramic analysis (E. Wyllys Andrews V writing on "The Early Ceramic History of the Lowland Maya"), or models of explaining ancient Maya subsistence patterns (Peter D. Harrison's contribution: "The Revolution in Ancient Maya Subsistence"). Some contributions deal with problems that were neglected in previous studies or present them in a completely different way (like Flora S. Clancy on "A Genealogy for Freestanding Maya Monuments" or Richard M. Leventhal's "Southern Belize: An Ancient Maya Region"), while other authors tend to give us state-of-the-art contributions that summarize working models present in this area of research since the early 1980s (paper on Lowland Maya wetland agriculture at Río Azul by T. Patrick Culbert, Laura J. Levi, and Luis Cruz, and the chapter on early architectural history of Mundo Perdido, Tikal, and its dynastic consequences by Juan Pedro Laporte and Vilma Fialko, and also Anthony P. Andrews's "The Role of Trading Ports in Maya Civilization"). Among the most interesting contributions are the ones dealing with transition from Classic to Postclassic in Northern Belize (by David M. Pendergast) and the brilliant ethnographic essay by Grant D. Jones on the sources that help us to better understand Maya colonial history.

In some sense, the structure of the book and the quality of the individual contributions justify the regional approach in Mesoamerican studies. This approach has also been employed in a recent publication on the Olmec culture and its contemporaries (for example, in Sharer and Grove's *Regional Perspectives on the Olmec*, 1989 – see also the first chapter in the present book) with great success. In the book presented here, its importance is not explicitly stressed (except, maybe, by Richard Leventhal [cf.

pp. 125-126]), but all the contributors start from the relatively limited (in both time and space) set of data from a certain area or site, and then try to expand these data further. Sometimes, data lead to questions that remain open (for example, the nature of the relationship between Seibal and Tikal posed by Clemency C. Coggins). It can also be argued that the starting points for the study are not always the best points from which to expand. For example, Linda Schele presents (as usual) a detailed study of dedication ceremonies and house names at Palenque. But what is the wider significance of her chapter if we know that Palenque is (geographically, politically, and especially epigraphically) an exception in the Lowland Maya area (cf. de la Garza 2007)? If so many exceptions in ancient Maya writing are encountered only at Palenque, is it valid to try to interpret the writings from other sites (which have little or no irregularity) using the information based on the examples from Palenque?

Another interesting thing to be noted is the inter-disciplinary approach, since the authors come from different fields: archaeology, art history, epigraphy, and ethnohistory. Within this interdisciplinary approach, there is a great emphasis on the iconography (papers by Laporte and Fialko, Freidel, Coggins, and Schele), and, at least in Freidel's case it is demonstrated in great detail how the ancient Maya symbols (in this case, the Jester god) changed and transformed over the time, with different cultural implications for the social organization from Preclassic into Postclassic. While the image might stay the same, its context and meaning significantly shift over the longer periods of time (Edmonson 1979; Estrada Belli 2006).

Preparing publications based on conferences is very often associated with the risk that some or most of the contributions will be out-of-date by the time that the book becomes available to the general public (in this case, more than four years have passed since the conference, and two years since the book was actually completed, in April of 1991). However, the editors, contributors, and the publisher did a great job by updating some of the chapters in the process, so that as a final product we have a nicely printed (with a lot of drawings, architectural reconstructions, and site plans) and very useful summary of the research since the early 1980s, but also a book that can pose important questions for future research. *Vision and Revision* is certainly open to criticism and revision(s), but at the moment of its publication, it is without any doubt a very important contribution to Maya archaeology.

6. Ancient Maya Politics and Ideology

Antonia E. Foias, *Ancient Maya Political Dynamics*. Gainesville: University Press of Florida, 2013. 290 pp.

Although the historical content in ancient Maya inscriptions was famously predicted as far back as in 1910 (by Charles P. Bowditch), it was taken seriously only in 1950s and 1960s by scholars like Tatiana Proskouriakoff and Heinrich Berlin (as well as Thompson 1961). These authors were followed by others, such as T. Patrick Culbert's study of "collapse" theories in the 1970s and more specific considerations of Maya state organization by archaeologists like R. E. W. Adams since 1981. Subsequent research and the decipherment of the Classic Maya inscriptions has led to a resurgence in interest in different aspects of ancient Maya political organization. Antonia E. Foias' book presents a very welcome addition to this growing field of study. Furthermore, the style of her work, which considers general accounts of the state (including anthropology of politics and studies of power in general) and adds to these considerations with the data from other parts of the world and comparable historical periods, makes this a book that is easy to read. The tables and illustrations serve to illuminate the author's main points. Foias' data are frequently drawn from Motul de San José (as the locality in the Petén in Guatemala is known today), where she recently directed a long-term project. The site was the seat a fascinating polity in the Southern Maya Lowlands, which apparently shifted its allegiance from Tikal to Calakmul, before being conquered by Dos Pilas.

The main text is subdivided into seven chapters. The "Introduction" presents some basic remarks about Mesoamerican chronology. The important point when discussing organization of ancient societies is that one should not take for granted some of the previous models, like the one of the "Asiatic mode of production," the model which was first suggested by Karl Marx, and in mid-20th century was elaborated by Karl A. Wittfogel. Quite to the contrary, as the author notes: "Maya people lived well at the site [of Motul de San José – A. B.] during the Late Classic period" (4). Of course, there is a risk into running into another extreme – the idea that premodern states were all about peace and harmony. Foias shows that this is also quite unlikely: "The reality of the past is that systems were predominately neither hierarchical nor equal; the truth lies somewhere in between, depending on local circumstances and historical contingencies" (5). The second and third chapters present brief but informative outlines of the relationship between political anthropology, archaeology, and the study of ancient states. For example, R. E. W. Adams' work in particular has drawn on possible analogies between medieval Yoruba city states and the Mesoamerican political organization, and in recent years, analogies have also been drawn with the states in ancient Southeast Asia. All of this puts the Classic Maya (as well as their neighbours) in a wider context of the development and adaptation of human cultures to their particular natural (ecological) and historical environment.

Chapters 4, 5, and 6 present different levels of political analysis, progressing from the macro- to the middle-, and micro-level. Foias first outlines the debates on whether Classic Maya polities were organized as "centralized," or "decentralized" states. It seems that part of the problem is that our understanding and use of these terms stems from the understanding of contemporary world, while the extent to which our "modern" terminology should be extended back in the past remains open. After presenting several case studies, Foias seems to side with Joyce Marcus' view that the most useful model for interpreting ancient Maya states is the "dynamic" one – not only did these states vary in shape and size, their alliances also changed over time, and were dependent on a number of factors. When discussing the internal organization of these states, Foias introduces welcome comparisons with China (Qin dynasty), using as her starting point Max Weber's classical study of bureaucracy (Weber 1946, Ch. VIII). She concludes that there are three main characteristics of Classic Maya political structure. Firstly, it "was political-ecclesiastical, and nobles were promoted from lower to higher positions during their lifetimes. Secondly, it was hierarchical, and there were from two to four levels of elite officials. Thirdly, it was intensely personal, and superior elite patrons 'owned' the lower officials or priests, even after death" (160 ff.). As political power also needed to be asserted in everyday life, this was done through numerous public rituals – which, of course, had their costs, meaning that political performances demanded "control over economic resources but not necessarily control over all of economy" (192). In tracing the lines of political influences, Foias uses both the latest advances in the decipherment of Maya glyphs and new assessments of Mayan economic practices, primarily related to trade and tribute. Different objects were used as tools for exercising and displaying power – she cites examples of figurines, pots, and stone monuments. (Perhaps her discussion of the role of ideology would also have benefited from considerations of the work of the French sociologist Raymond Aron.) Most importantly, the role of the so-called "commoners" should not be overlooked, as they were an integral part of the political landscape in which they played an active role.

In her "Conclusions," Foias claims that the "aim of this work is to present how archaeologists have reconstructed ancient Maya politics during the Classic period" (220). But this book is much more than that. It is an exemplary model of good scholarship and clearly presented arguments that should find an audience far beyond specialized Mesoamericanist courses.

7. Paletin's Discovery of the New World

Introduction

Ignacio Bernal's (1962) impressive annotated bibliography of the research in Mesoamerica between 1514 and 1960, completely omits works published in the territory of the former Yugoslavia – in particular, articles and books in Serbo-Croatian[5] and Slovenian. This should be attributed mostly to the relative inaccessibility of these languages to scholars engaged in Middle American research, especially regarding pre-Columbian cultures. People who have working knowledge of these languages are mostly engaged in linguistics, history, or Old World (especially Neolithic and late Roman) archaeology. They appear to have been much less interested in anthropology and ethnology, the disciplines that produced most of the Americanist research in this century.

Naturally, a short chapter can not remedy this great discrepancy. What I intend to do is to present a brief overview of the works dealing with the pre-Columbian civilizations in Middle America in Serbo-Croatian, and Slovenian until late 1990s, and then focus on one of the participants of the conquest of Yucatán, Vinko Paletin. As I am not going to cover the most recent research in these languages, I will not deal in this chapter with probably the most widely known and respected scholar from the region, Slovenian archaeoastronomer Ivan Šprajc (2001, 2009).

An Overview of Research

The first series of articles dealing with Middle American Indians in Croatia appeared in four consecutive issues of the *Catholic Journal* (*Katolički list*)[6] in Zagreb in 1885 under the same title, "Bartolomé de Las Casas and the Indians' Struggle for Freedom" (Jambrušić 1885). These articles introduced the great mid-1550s debates between Las Casas and Ginés de Sepúlveda to the general public in Croatia. It is interesting to note that this publication appear when Croatia was still part of the Austro-Hungarian Empire during a time when Croatian nationalism was on the rise. In that context, introducing the discussions dealing with the human rights of conquered populations in other continents and ethnic backgrounds does seem curious and might have served the purposes of Croatian nationalists in their struggle for self-determination.

In any case, the interest for Middle America did spread to other parts of the Austro-Hungarian Empire, and in 1890 in Novi Sad, R. Žeravica published in the journal *Banner* (*Zastava*) the article "The Ruins in Mexico." This article seems to be an eclectic

---

[5] I decided to use the most commonly (socio-linguistically) accepted name of the language as it was known in the former Yugoslavia, without any political overtones or implications. In Bosnia and Herzegovina, the language is today called Bosnian, in Croatia – Croatian, in Montenegro – Montenegrin, and in Serbia – Serbian. In the original version of this paper, published in 1997, I used the terms "Croatian" and "Serbian."
[6] When mentioning specific publications I will put the original name of the publication (in Serbo-Croatian or Slovenian) in brackets.

combination of observations from the author's own journey to Mexico and other descriptions published by 1880s (especially the ones from the Maya area, since he did not travel there) by other scholars.

The increasing immigration from the Balkan Peninsula by the end of the 19th century also increased the presence of South Slavs throughout the Latin America. Most people came in search of a better life for themselves and their families. Some were also adventurers and explorers. Among the latter, especially interesting are the Seljan brothers (Lazarević 1977), and for the subject of this paper it should be noted that Stevo Seljan left a short manuscript under the title "Curiosities of Central America," written probably around 1908.

After the unification of Serbs, Croats, and Slovenians in a single state (in 1918), the interest in this subject was expressed first in the article on the "Decline of the Maya Kingdom" (Tomičić 1935) in the Zagreb journal *Family* (*Obitelj*) - an eclectic article drawing heavily on the research done up to that date.

A few years later (1937), Debeljak writes in Slovenian on "The Aztec Culture."[7] After the Second World War, Melita Viličić (1953) wrote a treatise on pre-Columbian architecture. Her text consisted of several chapters originally prepared for the general history of architecture that were eventually published as a separate volume.

Due to ideological reasons (affiliation with Communist ideology, the dominant component of the cultural life in Yugoslavia from 1945 until its dissolution in 1991), Knorozov's work on Maya hieroglyphs was easily introduced in the several volumes dealing with the origins of writing. This influence survived much later in the works of the Momčilović brothers in Belgrade. Actually, the older brother, Vladimir Momčilović, focused his work (he was a freelance researcher in the Belgrade's City Committee of the Communist Party) on the role and influence of the Catholic Church in Latin America, but this did not prevent him from discussing other issues, as when he criticized other authors for their neglect of Russian scholarship (Momčilović 1988; the reply is in Bošković 1989c).

Probably the most important event of the 1980s was the introduction of the splendour of the Mesoamerican civilizations through a series of translations. These actually began to appear with B. Prelević's translation of the León-Portilla's *Los antiguos mexicanos a través de sus crónicas y cantares* (in 1979). This trend continued with the translations (in all cases, from Spanish – *not* from the original manuscripts) by Lj. Ristanović of the Recinos version of the "Popol Vuh" (1983a), then Barrera Vásquez and Rendón edition of "El libro de los libros de Chilam Balam" (1983b), and the new (at the time, Robert M. Carmack's) version of "Título de Totonicapan" (1984).[8] All three titles were published by

---

[7] My data on research in Slovenian are too fragmentary, so I mention only this article as an illustration of the early interest in the subject and (to my knowledge) the first article on Mesoamerica published in Slovenian language.

[8] The editor and translator noted that it was the first edition of this text anywhere in the world, and he also acknowledged the help of Carmack – who found this text in the Guatemala highlands. This is a rather

the Bagdala Publishing House from Kruševac (Serbia), a local publisher who specialized in Third World literatures. The translator acknowledged the help of René Acuña and Robert Carmack, but still, his commentaries remained rather confused, fragmentary, and perplexing for a person without background in ancient Mesoamerican cultures. (Which, in the case of his readership at the time, meant everyone.)

Finally, my own work was primarily oriented towards understanding and interpretation of ancient Mesoamerican civilizations through their religions (Bošković 1986a, 1986b, 1988a, 1988b, 1989b, 1990). This included a paper in the highly prestigious *Bulletin of the Ethnographical Institute of the Serbian Academy of Sciences and Arts* (Boskovic 1988b). Approximately at the same time I edited (1989) a selection of articles (in translation) by Beatriz de la Fuente (1972), David C. Grove (1973), and Ulrich Köhler on the "Olmec" (1985), and wrote a brief introduction to the oral literature of the Maya Indians for a Belgrade-based literary magazine (1989b).

Las Casas and the Conquest of the Americas

As already noted above, the first articles in Serbo-Croatian on pre-Columbian Middle America dealt in great detail with the life and times of Bartolomé de Las Casas (1474-1566), traditionally regarded as a symbol (or at least, a figure of immense importance) of the struggle for dignity of American Indians (Šanjek 1978, 1991). Actually, Las Casas can be seen (in a historical context) as a continuation of the efforts of his fellow Dominicans, Antonio de Montesinos and Pedro de Córdoba, who were already refusing to hear the confessions of Spanish settlers at Santo Domingo (Haiti), due to what they considered to be inhuman treatment of the native population. Las Casas went a little further by soliciting the abolition of *encomiendas* and *repartimientos*[9] as iredeemably evil and immoral. In the letter to king Carlos V in 1516, he wrote that it is better to lose all the lands overseas than to allow that such horrible injustices be done in the name of the king. With the support of Dominican theologians from the University of Salamanca, Las Casas eventually succeeded (with considerable help from the Spanish royalty) in arguing for laws that abolished *encomiendas* and granted freedom (at least formally, if not in practice) to the native population in 1542.

Among the most notable of his fellow Dominicans were Bartolomé de Carranza, Melchior Cano, and Domingo de Soto. They attempted to prove that Pope Alexander's VI 1493 bull "Inter caetera" was valid only in the spiritual sense – giving to the Spanish and the Portuguese the right to Christianize native population in the territories that they discover, but not to treat these territories and their inhabitants as their own property. The Dominican General, Thomas de Caeta, wrote in his commentary to the edition of the *Summa theologica* of Thomas Aquinas that there were actually three kinds of infidels: 1) the ones that were legally and factually subjects of the Christians and

---

extraordinary event, since most of his commentaries to the other texts are usually just translations of other people's comments (for the "Popol Vuh," for example, the ones by Adrian Recinos) – without any references.

[9]   Without getting into a detailed explanation of these important Colonial institutions, I will only say that they refer to a series of regulations that basically connected (tied) native inhabitants to the lands that were purchased by settlers or given away as gifts, thus keeping the native population practically as slaves.

lived in the Christian kingdoms (Moors, Jews); 2) the ones that were legally but not factually Christian subjects because they seized Christian territories (Turks); and 3) the ones that were neither legally nor factually Christian subjects (Indians). He concluded that the second kind (Turks) should be treated like enemies, but that the third kind (Indians) was a legal owner of their own lands and should not be subjected to force. These and similar statements were recognized in the bull of Pope Paul III, "Sublimus Deus," of June 2, 1537:

> Desiring to provide ample remedy for these evils [persecution and killing of the native population by the conquistadors – A. B.], We define and declare by these Our letters, or by any translation thereof signed by any notary public and sealed with the seal of any ecclesiastical dignitary, to which the same credit shall be given as to the originals, that, notwithstanding whatever may have been or may be said to the contrary, the said Indians and all other people who may later be discovered by Christians, are by no means to be deprived of their liberty or the possession of their property, even though they be outside the faith of Jesus Christ; and that they may and should, freely and legitimately, enjoy their liberty and the possession of their property; nor should they be in any way enslaved; should the contrary happen, it shall be null and have no effect (after Gutierrez 1878: 428-429).[10]

However, the theoretical question of the justification for the use of force in converting the native population to the "true faith" and the "true God" had already been raised by a lawyer from Córdoba, Juan Ginés de Sepúlveda, in his treatise "Démocrates alter sive de iustis belli causis" (Rome 1535). Sepúlveda stressed the fact that the Indians were, in his opinion, "infidels, barbarians, and slaves by their very nature" (quoted in Coe, Snow & Benson 1986: 22). All of this led to the famous discussion between him and Las Casas in 1548 at Valladolid in Spain. In this debate, Las Casas claimed that the differentiation of the civilized peoples and the barbarians could not be based on ethnic, cultural, and religious differences, but on the fact that there are people that respect liberties, freedom and natural rights of the others and people that do not respect these rights. Although the royal auditors never officially declared the outcome of this debate, the fact that shortly after it (in 1552) Las Casas was granted permission to publish his *Brevísima relación de la destruición de las Indias* (2006), while Ginés de Sepúlveda never received official sanction to publish his polemical works,[11] speaks for itself.

Vinko Paletin: Looking for the Compromise

However, views expressed by Las Casas and other Dominicans were not enthusiastically embraced in the New World. In this context, we encounter Vinko Paletin (1508-1573), a native of the island of Korčula, in the Adriatic Sea off central Dalmatian coast of Croatia. At the age of 20 he left his native island for Spain (Šanjek 1978, 1991). Eventually, he

---

[10] Original in Latin available at Wikisource at: https://la.wikisource.org/wiki/Sublimis_Deus

[11] His account of the debate in Valldolid was only published in the 19th century. It is interesting to note that his arguments were used by Bernal Díaz del Castillo (1494/8-1584), in his account of the "True History of the Conquest of New Spain," finished in 1568. Following Ginés de Sepúlveda, he claimed that the war waged against the Indians was a "just war."

became a sailor and left for the New World in 1535, where he participated in the conquest of Yucatán, under the command of the younger Francisco de Montejo (between 1535 and 1541). He became a Dominican during his stay in Mexico between 1542 and 1543 (Šanjek 1978, 1991). After his return to Europe, he studied theology (in Bologna, 1546-1552), compiled a map of Spain (1550), translated Pedro de Medina's "L'arte del navegar," into Italian, wrote a treatise (now lost) "De la institución del buen gobierno" (1560), wrote a short description of the Yucatán, and taught mathematics and cosmography at the Academy at Vicenza (from 1560). A much more detailed account is in Šanjek (1978).

However, his most famous work is a treatise in Spanish and Latin "On the Right and Necessity of War That Is Being Waged by the Spanish Kings against the Peoples of the West Indies," written in 1557/1558.[12] In this treatise, Paletin summarized the main arguments of both the conquerors and their opponents, taking as his starting point the rebuttal of the writings of Las Casas, which he describes as "insulting and harmful" (Šanjek 1978: 102). Trying to choose the middle way between what he saw as two extremes, Paletin noted that the Indians are much more likely to be traitors and liars, and to commit sins against nature, and to sacrifice other human beings than to live a life of virtue. However, unlike his more famous Dominican contemporaries, he did believe that the Indians could be brought to civilized life by force. In his final arguments it seems that the Paletin the conquistador defeated Paletin the Dominican.

The Maya Civilization of the Yucatán Peninsula, as seen by Paletin

The content of this treatise is mostly known to us from the secondary sources – only some fragments still remain today, and they are kept in the Dominican monastery in Korčula. Two versions of this text exist outside Korčula, both incomplete and dating from the 18th century. The Manuscript Phillipps Ind. 11798 (in Latin) is housed in the library of the Indiana University in Bloomington, while the other copy, the Spanish version, discovered by J. B. Muñoz on January 21, 1784, is in the Archivo General de las Indias in Sevilla. The latter one was published in Hanke and Millares Carlo (1943: 12-37) and is the basis of the Croatian edition. In what follows, I use the Croatian edition, which is more accurate and takes into account other (primarily Latin) contemporary sources.

One of the most fascinating (and most complete) fragments contains Paletin's brief description of Yucatán, with remarks that the marvellous cities were, according to the natives, built by a race of bearded people resembling Spaniards who were eventually defeated by the Mayas and had to leave their cities, leaving them empty as they were on the eve of the conquest. Paletin was convinced that the pyramids and temples that he saw were actually built by the Carthaginians, since the notion of an autochthonous, Indian civilization was something completely unacceptable at the time. Here is what he wrote:

---

[12] The Croatian translation (by I. Mihojević) is published in Šanjek 1978: 102-127. Although some fragments have been published, only Šanjek 1978 has the full version of the ones that were preserved.

The Yucatan peninsula has several provinces. One is Zacatlan, a little bit more than a day's walk from the sea, with the old structure of finely worked stone and a high tower. In the middle is the temple where they made sacrifices to their idols, and the Indians call this temple *cu*. (...)

Another province is called Ciciniza [Chichén Itzá] where, I believe, New Salamanca had been founded. (...) The Indians annoyed us and we had to leave that place where remnants of the old structures are still visible. There are also seven towers, but the Indians do not live there. On all these structures and towers there are images of infantry and soldiers, bearded and with armour, helmets, and other objects; they have sharp swords, darts, and axes. There are also the Amazons there, and everything is depicted like an army that is on the move. Two rows of letters were on these towers, but none of us could understand them. They were not Latin, or Greek, or Hebrew. As far as I can tell, these letters are from Africa, from Carthage. The letters are still there today, and your Majesty [the treatise is addressed to the king Philip II] can determine what language they represent. Right next to that tower there is a wonderful stream and all around there are many old fruit trees.

Some among us, the ones who were more curious, while admiring the structures, repeatedly asked the Indians what were these structures for, these old and ruined cities that existed long ago. They all replied that they have heard from their forefathers that many years ago bearded people came with ships from afar, just as you [the Spaniards] come (...) and they founded these cities and lived in them. As time went by, the ships and the people stopped coming. When our [Yucatec Mayan] forefathers saw that, they started attacking them. They wore them down with hunger and war, killed and destroyed them. The cities were left empty and in ruins, and they still remain that way.

It is quite obvious that everything fits: history, the position of this land, distance of this land from the Europe and Africa, remnants of buildings.

It seems that in the beginning these territories were Carthaginian and Roman. After that, the Catholic kings [of Spain], eager to spread the Divine Word more than other Christian kings, with all the expenses, did everything [in order] to discover these territories under the command of the Captain Cristóbal Colón [Christopher Columbus]. As a supreme arbiter of all the kings, the Pope has legally announced that these formerly Roman lands now belong to the Spanish kings, which conquered them according to the justice and law and kept them under their command. (quoted in Šanjek 1978: 120 ff.; also Šanjek 1991).

Concluding Remarks

I believe that the preserved fragments of Paletin's text could help us to further understand the on-going theoretical battles (at the time of the Conquest) over the lives and property of the American Indians, as well as some of the very earthly concerns that were involved. Obviously, a view of the participants in the conquest was sharply different from the view of the clergy that tried to – within their powers – protect the native population.

Furthermore, Paletin is one of the first authors that tried to rationally explain the origin of the magnificent structures that the conquerors saw in the abandoned cities. Certainly, Carthage is a very wild guess, but we must understand that to admit that the "inferior" and "barbaric" native population could have built something like Chichén Itzá was completely impossible for the conquerors. Any notion that the natives had a high civilization of their own seemed quite impossible. Therefore, authors were examining the arguments and looking for the most rational solutions. Voilá, here is Carthage.

This is also one of the earliest accounts on the Maya hieroglyphic writing (written before Diego de Landa's *Relación de las cosas de Yucatán*), although not the earliest (Coe 1989). I do believe that some similar surprises await us in the course of examining early Colonial records of the New World. Maybe there are many more Paletins, with works less fragmented and more precise, that need to enter the field of our scholarly research.

8. Codex Borbonicus

Introduction

Codex Borbonicus or, more accurately, *Codex Cihuacoatl* (Anders, Jansen and Reyes Garcia 1991; also Jansen and Pérez Jiménez 2004), is one of the most beautiful and probably the largest surviving ancient Mexican manuscript. It was painted on one side of paper made from the bark of the fig tree (in Nahuatl: *amatl*), although both sides were prepared for painting with a thin layer of a mineral paste. Technically speaking, the document is not really a codex but a unique document that folds like an accordion, made of paper that was originally set up in 40 (forty) parts (pages or tables). Of these, 36 "pages" of the screenfold still exist, while the first two and the last two are missing. Each "page" is between 39 and 40 square centimetres large, and the length of the whole manuscript before the loss of four pages was 15.8 meters (Codex Borbonicus 1974). Kubler mistakenly put the size of the pages as 28 by 28 centimetres (Kubler 1984), while the Graz (1974) edition is 39 by 40 centimetres, making it slightly larger than the original.

Little is known about the manuscript before it was acquired by the library of the Chambre des Députés in Paris (now the Assemblée Nationale). Donald Robertson (1959) wrote, following del Paso y Troncoso (1979: 30-36), that it was mentioned for the first time in the second edition of William Robertson's *History of America* (Robertson 1777). At the time, it was allegedly in a library in Escorial in Spain (Glass 1975: 21). However, whether William Robertson actually saw the manuscript remains uncertain – in his very detailed commentary on the Codex Hamy does not mention him at all (*Codex Borbonicus* 1899). It is generally assumed that it was brought to France from Spain by Napoleon's soldiers (Glass and Robertson 1975: 97-98). The Library of the Chambre des Députés bought it for 1300 francs in May 1826 (Hamy in *Codex Borbonicus* 1899: 1-2). J.-F. Waldeck saw it while working on the project of copying ancient Mexican manuscripts financed by Lord Kingsborough, but he was not allowed to copy it (Glass and Robertson 1975: 97).

The manuscript is mentioned for the first time in a letter by the Librarian of the Assembly, Joseph Marius Alexis Aubin, dated 6 January 1841. This letter is reproduced in Aubin's text published in 1859. After that, the "Codex" was exhibited for six months during the World Exposition in Paris in 1876. It was published for the first time in 1899, as part of the project funded by Duc de Loubat, in the photolithographic edition that rendered the original colours very accurately. It is interesting to note that Glass (1975: 25) never mentions Loubat's financing of this edition, even though this is quite obvious from the edition itself. It is also interesting that this edition (as well as the one of del Paso y Troncoso 1979/1898) has Arabic numbers in the upper right hand corners of all pages. This pagination has since been deleted, so it was not present in the original, nor in the 1974 and 1991 reproductions. This edition includes Hamy's commentary – probably still the most detailed and most complete commentary on the manuscript (although the most accurate is probably the one by Anders, Jansen and Reyes García 1991).

A hand-painted edition of 25 copies was published in Mexico in 1938. It is difficult to understand the motive for this, as the pages (based on the 1899 edition) are copied so badly that they resemble a children's colouring book. The colours hardly resemble the colours of the original. In late 1940, a partial edition (pages 3 to 20, as black-and-white photographs) was published in New York, together with Vaillant's brief and very eclectic commentary on the 260 day ritual calendar, *tonalamatl*. Finally, a photographic reproduction was published in Graz in 1974. Although Nowotny's commentary in this version is perhaps too brief (it is a description of the manuscript's content), the codicological description by Jacqueline de Durand-Forest is exceptional. This edition was slightly revised (with new commentaries added) in 1991 – and it remains the best edition for scholarly use. In her Catalog, Martha Barton Robertson (1991) mentioned only the last edition.

A photographic reproduction of the 1899 edition was printed in Mexico in 1979, together with the very detailed 1898 study by del Paso y Troncoso, as well as with a translation of Hamy's 1899 commentary.

There are some controversies regarding the dating of the manuscript, considering its style, clear colours, and the absence of any meaningful commentary in Spanish (on the manuscript itself). There is a general consensus that it dates from the Early Colonial period. Robertson claimed that it was painted before 1541, although some authors (Hamy, del Paso y Troncoso, Caso, Lizardi Ramos, Apenes) believed it to be of pre-Conquest origin. In his classic study of Pre-Hispanic calendars, Caso (1967) rejected Robertson's claim. Quiñones Keber (2006) accepts the probable time of its painting as the 1520s, putting it approximately at the time of the conquest.

There were also some uncertainties regarding the geographic origin of this codex. Most early commentators assumed it to be of the Aztec origin (that is to say, that it was created in Tenochtitlán or its immediate vicinity), but Nicholson (1974), based on, among other things, prominent displays of the goddess Cihuacoatl, suggested Culhuacán or Iztapalapa to the south – an idea also supported by Quiñones Keber (1988: 210). However, the two of them seem to be unique in this suggestion. After a careful analysis of style, Robertson (1959) concluded that it was painted in Tenochtitlán, together with three other manuscripts. In support of his thesis, Brown (1977: 223) pointed to the similarity of the day signs to the ones present in the *Codex Mendoza*. According to Kubler (1990: 113), *Codex Borbonicus* and *Codex Telleriano-Remensis* represent examples of the school of painting that was led by the Franciscans in the 16th century that was based in Tenochtitlán and Tlatelolco. This school is characterized by manuscripts painted with large figures in more or less cursive style. Considering its style and content, Jansen and Pérez Jiménez assume that the manuscript was painted in Xochimilco, and put it within what they call a "Borgia Group," or "Books of Wisdom" (2004: 269-270).

The Content of the Manuscript

The Codex has four distinctive sections (Glass and Robertson 1975: 97-98). The first part consists of pages 3-20, or the *tonalamatl*, the description of the 260 day ritual calendar (which also served as a kind of manual for diviners), with deities presiding over different days, signs for these days and their numbers, sequences of nine Lords of the Night and thirteen Lords of the Day, as well as the "birds" (i.e., anything that can fly – including butterflies) associated with different days. This portion of the Codex is quite worn out, which points to the fact that it might have been painted before the rest of the manuscript – or it was simply used much more than other parts. Quiñones Keber dedicated a study to this part only (1987).

The second part is formed by pages 21 and 22, with representations of Lords of the Night associated with certain numbers and "yearbearers" of the 52 year cycles, with large mythical figures in the middle of the pages. This part has been studied extensively (Lizardi Ramos 1953; Apenes 1953; Caso 1953, 1967; Burland 1957; Kubler 1984), and I will return to it later.

The third part consists of pages 23 to 37, divided into 19 parts, which represent a yearly cycle of festivities. This part has been analysed by Couch (1985), and a good comparative overview has been provided by Quiñones Keber (1988). According to her, in a more recent summary:

> The second major section of the screenfold depicts ritual scenes associated with the eighteen annual ceremonies of the solar year, which consisted of eighteen twenty-day periods that the Spaniards called *veintenas* (23–37). Each one was dedicated to a particular deity or deities and featured an attendant set of ritual activities centering on agricultural and social concerns. Engaged in the pertinent rituals are costumed deity impersonators, priests, musicians, and ordinary, simply garbed commoners. Figures are well and colorfully drawn but smaller in scale than the dominant deity figures of the *tonalamatl*. Scale is sometimes arbitrary, for example, a subsidiary image (e.g., a clay pot with offerings) drawn larger than a nearby human participant. In contrast to the rigid grid of the *tonalamatl*, with its hieratic supernaturals, the *veintena* section lacks a consistent organizational plan for representing the varied activities carried out at major temple sites and other locales. The eighteen scenes are distributed among fourteen panels, with some panels divided by drawn black lines to accommodate more than one scene and some scenes extending across panel folds. Some scenes read vertically, whereas others are painted sideways, requiring the viewer to turn the panel (and entire screenfold) to view them. Scenes also vary in detail; some are sparsely depicted, with few participants, whereas others are more complex, with crowded fields and sequential activities. These inconsistencies also suggest a post-Conquest date, because pre-Conquest manuscripts from other areas are more uniformly organized and drawn. Although a few other *veintena* cycles survive, none displays the richness of the *Codex Borbonicus* episodes. These vivid scenes convey the remarkable panoply that characterized these lively and colorful public ceremonies, which were carried out with music, dancing, feasting, processions, costumed performers, and sacrificial offerings. (Quiñones Keber 2006)

Finally, the fourth part consists of pages 37 and 38 and begins with the same image as page 23. Taking into account the information in the (now lost) last two pages, it could be assumed with a degree of certainty that this part included representations of deities that dominated the 52 year cycles. It seems that this was the most important part of the manuscript. The symbol of the ceremony of lighting the "New Fire" is above the first date written on this page. The New Fire ceremony marked the re-creation of the world, and it was the ceremony that marked the beginning of the new 52 year cycle. A good early study of this part of the Codex was done by Brown (1977: 226-229, table 21), preceding a much more detailed analysis by Jansen (in Anders, Jansen and Reyes García 1991).

Deities of the Codex Cihuacoatl

One of the main characteristics of this screenfold is the quality of the paintings. All the large mythic figures are painted in the first two sections of the codex, and they represent some of the most beautiful images of Mexica deities that we have.

Figure 3 depicts page 11 of the *tonalamatl*. The large figure represents a Central Mexican earth goddess Cihuacoatl ("Snake Woman"), one of the most important Mexica Aztec

FIG. 3. PAGE 13 OF THE CODEX, WITH THE GODDESS CIHUACOATL (IN HER ASPECT AS TLAZOLTEOTL).

female deities, in her aspect as the goddess who oversees childbirth (González Torres 1991: 38-39). Square representations [in figure 3] should be read in the following order: first the lower horizontal seven, then the inside vertical six (representing day signs, numbers, and sequence of the nine Lords of the Night), the upper horizontal seven, and finally the outer vertical six (representing thirteen Lords of the Day and the "birds" associated with them. The complete sequence of this 13-day period, which formed part of the 260 day ritual calendar, known as *tonalpohualli* among the Mexicas, is the following:

Day	Lord of the Night	Lord of the Day	Bird
1 *ollin*	Centeotl	Xiuhtecutli	White hummingbird
2 *tecpatl*	Mictlantecuhtli	Tlaltecutli	Green hummingbird
3 *quiauitl*	Chalchihuitlicue	Chalchihuitlicue	Falcon
4 *xochitl*	Tlazolteotl	Tonatiuh	Quail
5 *cipactli*	Tepeyollotl	Tlazolteotl	Eagle
6 *ehecatl*	Tlaloc	Teoyaomiqui	Owl
7 *calli*	Xiuhtecutli	Xochipilli	Butterfly
8 *cuetzpallin*	Itztli	Tlaloc	Striped eagle
9 *coatl*	Piltzintecutli	Ehecatl	Turkey
10 *miquiztli*	Centeotl	Tezcatlipoca	Horned owl
11 *mazatl*	Mictlantecutli	Mictlantecutli	Guacamaya
12 *tochtli*	Chalchihuitlicue	Tlahuizcalpantecutli	Quetzal
13 *atl*	Tlazolteotl	Ilamatecutli	Parrot

This period is governed by Cihuacoatl (perhaps in her aspect as the goddess of childbirth, Tlazolteotl), so she is surrounded by objects and symbols associated with her.

The next illustration (Figure 4) represents the "New Fire" ceremony (cf. Brundage 1985: 36ff). This important event marked the re-creation of the original creation of the present world. Thus it marked the end of the ancient Mexican 52 year period of time ("century"). The rituals connected with the end of 52 year cycles were very important throughout Mesoamerica. It is unclear whether the actual lighting of the fire takes place here – Nicholson claimed that it seems that the central scene depicts the events *immediately following* the "New Fire" ceremony, after which new fires were distributed throughout the region. There are numerous characters in this wonderful and quite realistically depicted image, but they are all at different points in time. The depictions along the margins show the events *before* the ceremony. Two families (right and lower right hand side) eagerly await the outcome of the ceremony, and their faces are covered with blue masks (that almost look like clouds near their faces). There is also a warrior guarding a pregnant woman (he is ready, just in case, for it was also believed that during these rituals women can transform into wild creatures that will devour anything that they find), and people depicted on the right hand side obviously do not know whether the ceremony was successful. The sign at the upper left side is *ome acatl* (2 Reed), which points to the last "New Fire" ceremony before the conquest, corresponding to 1507 CE in our calendar.

Fig. 4. pages 21-22, with Oxomoco and Cipactonal (top), and Quetzalcoatl and
Tezcatlipoca (bottom).

As noted above, pages 21 and 22 have been studied extensively. Kubler noted that they connect two different parts of the manuscript, *tonalamatl* on the one side and the description of periodic ceremonies on the other. They also connect the section that has been worn out, with the part that depicts some scenes in a Colonial style (the most famous example is the depiction of the ritual dance around the *xocotl* pole, on page 28 right). Both pages are done in a similar way: each of them depicts the 26 year sequence with deities who preside over these years, along with Lords of the Night (Kubler 1984: 134). Large figures at the centre of both pages serve to justify the cosmogonic implications of the Central Mexican calendar round (the 52 year period), as well as the time calculation associated with it.

These large figures are well known deities. On page 22, Quetzalcoatl and Tezcatlipoca are depicted in some kind of a ritual dance. There are numerous myths about their role in the creation of the world (León-Portilla 1971, 1980; Brundage 1979: 31ff). Although in some versions they are adversaries, they usually cooperate in the creation of the world. Quetzalcoatl wears a duckbill mask, which identifies him as wind god Ehecatl (who has another aspect as the Night Wind, Yoalli Ehecatl). The idea of gods representing other gods is not very common, although the concept of human impersonators of deities is one of the fundamental concepts of Central Mexican religions (Hvidtfeldt 1958, Thompson 1933). Ethnohistorical sources point to the important role that both of these gods had in the years immediately before the conquest. Tezcatlipoca was associated with numerous war deities (Ixquimilli, Yaotl), but also with gods of song and dance – especially in his aspect as Huehuecóyotl ("Old Coyote"). This aspect is also very positive, since for the inhabitants of Central Mexico coyote epitomized the mundane wisdom and the capacity to easily get out of trouble. On the other hand, "Quetzalcoatl was the only Aztec god with enough human characteristics to be idealized" (Brundage 1979: 102), and in one of the creation myth versions he represents another aspect of Tezcatlipoca.

This apparently complicated system of relations between deities becomes a bit less complex if one focuses on the left side of the page 21. There, Oxomoco and Cipactonal are depicted as a pair of old deities, perhaps as Quetzalcoatl's and Tezcatlipoca's "mother" and "father." It is unclear why some of the more popular creation couples are not depicted in the screenfold. Perhaps this is one of the representations of the Lord of Duality, the double creator god Ometeotl, who lives with his consort, Omeyocan, in the highest sky and determines the fate of the world (León-Portilla 1971: 485, also León-Portilla 1999)? Perhaps this looks too much like a Eurocentric vision of the only true god who dominated ancient Mexico? As far as I am aware, Brundage (1979) is the only scholar who studied the role of Oxomoco and Cipactonal as creator gods in Central Mexican religions. Oxomoco's name literally means "the first woman," and it seems to derive from the Huastec (Meza 1981). It seems that this creator couple is a relatively late product, close to the time of the Spanish conquest, but so are the dancing Tezcatlipoca and Quetzalcoatl/ Ehecatl. Why are these deities depicted in such a prominent place? Could this help determine the function of this codex?

Possible Functions of the Manuscript

Several scholars (Robertson 1959, Brown 1979) suggested that the two halves of the codex were painted at different time (Couch 1985: 5). The idea that the Spanish conquerors commissioned the manuscript does not seem very likely considering that parts of the text were supposed to serve as reminders to the ones who painted it and to no one else. Almost all parts of the text (written by at least three different people) in the first part of the manuscript are completely unrelated to the actual content of the pages. On the other hand, the space that was left in the upper left hand corner of the pages of *tonalamatl* suggests that something was supposed to be added there. Couch suggested that, if the screenfold had been commissioned by a European buyer and it was never delivered, it is possible that it stayed a while among the local population. "In the society in which the calendar was not overseen by a central religious authority any more, *Borbonicus* would represent a perfect tool for recording both *tonalpohuallis* and yearly cycles" (Couch 1985: 5). Finally, Couch also explores a possibility that the manuscript was painted for local use only and commissioned by a local (Mexican) dignitary (1985: 5-6).

Taking into account the size of the screenfold, it is highly unlikely that it would have been carried around, although the worn out parts suggest that it might have been used over a longer period of time, perhaps during the ceremonies of giving names to new-born babies and similar ritual occasions which called for the use of calendar. The style, the beauty, and the content of the *Codex Cihuacoatl*, which looks almost like a general overview of the Aztec calendar rituals, point to its possible origin as a *nativistic document* created at the time of the conquest. It contains much more than the description of days, festivals, and presiding deities – it is a document that provides an outline of the whole cultural heritage that determined daily lives of the local population long before the European conquest. That is why it had to contain prophecies and predictions of ceremonies related to the 260 and 365 day cycles, as well as complex calculations with two dual representations of deities (Oxomoco and Cipactonal – Quetzalcoatl and Tezcatlipoca). Unfortunately for the creators of this magnificent document, it was already too late for the civilization that it represented to be resurrected as a living model. It was also too late to bring back the Mexica Aztec rule.

I believe that the depiction of deities and meanings associated with them could help understand why this manuscript was among the ones sent to the king of Spain Philip II, as "a large book about the chiefs of Mexico and the days to which they offered sacrifices during the week" ("*libro en folio mayor, de los caciques de México y de los días que sacrificaban en la semana*" (quoted in Jansen and Pérez Jiménez 2004: 270). Following this line of interpretation, it would perhaps be useful to interpret it from the perspective of nativism, as defined by Edmonson: "Nativism is the attempt to revive or perpetuate cultural traditions which a given group of people want to call 'their own' – with which they choose to identify themselves" (1960: 183-184). A ritual calendar was one of the main characteristics of Pre-Columbian cultures of Mesoamerica. It seems that the

Codex Cihuacoatl played an important role among segments of the local population in the decades after the conquest, and I am convinced that its influence should also be considered from a nativistic point of view – as a form of resistance to the Conquest. This manuscript is too unusual to be interpreted only as a wish of the conquerors to find out a little bit more about the people they have conquered.

Part Two – Myths, Dreams, and Religions

9. Religions of Mesoamerica

David Carrasco, *Religions of Mesoamerica: Cosmovision and Ceremonial Centers.* San Francisco: Harper and Row Publishers, 1990. xxviii+ 174 pp., illus., maps, photos.

This rather brief but important text introduces religious traditions of the areas of the New World where high civilizations were flourishing at least two millennia before the European contact. The emphasis is on the best known and (at the time of the writing of this book) best documented cultures of the Classic Maya (300-900 CE) and Aztecs (1325-1521 CE) and, to a much lesser extent, on the "Olmec" (ca. 1200-300 BCE), Teotihuacán (ca. 100-650 CE), and Toltec (ca. 900-1100 CE). Unfortunately, very little or no attention has been paid to the religious traditions of Oaxaca (Zapotec and Mixtec), as well as the Totonac and Huastec along the western coast of the Gulf of Mexico.

The book is divided into five chapters. The Introduction outlines what the author calls "inventions and fantasies of Mesoamerica," but it also includes a section on the sources for our understanding of Mesoamerica, as well as a very valuable section on the author's methodological approach. Davíd Carrasco considers religious traditions from this part of the world in terms of "Worldmaking, Worldcentering, Worldrenewing," with the strong emphasis on the important contribution of the Mexican historian Alfredo López Austin on the symbolism of the human body (López Austin 1980) and geographer's Paul Wheatley (1921-1999) on sacred geography. Professor Carrasco approaches study of Mesoamerican religions not from anthropology but from a more general perspective on the history of religions. This gives him the great advantage of incorporating the concept of *Religionswissenschaft* into the actual archaeological, ethnohistorical, and ethnological data, as well as the possibility of incorporating what is known from other disciplines, such as architecture and its notion of the sacred centre.

The next chapter gives an overview of the religious traditions mentioned above in chronological order, from "Olmec" to Aztec (or Mexica), emphasizing what the author sees as the universally Mesoamerican concept of the world and its ritual and ceremonial implications. It could be objected that not much attention is paid to regional variants, especially among the ancient Maya, where, for example, the data from Palenque could not explain with any degree of certainty mythic/religious histories of other cities, like Tikal, Calakmul, Lamanai, or Copán. Carrasco is at his best in the third chapter of the book, on the Aztec religion – after all, this is the subject on which he is the leading world authority. The next chapter is dedicated to the Classic Maya religion (including divine kingship, trials of the Underworld, etc.), and the fifth and final chapter concludes with a brilliant discussion of Mesoamerican religions after contact.

The book certainly serves its purpose "to help us understand and appreciate Mesoamerican religions" (157). This topic has fascinated scholars for over a century (Schellhas 1904, Hvidtfeldt 1958, Rivera Dorado 1986, De la Fuente 1972, Grove 1973, Brundage 1979, Hultkrantz 1979, León-Portilla 1987, 1999), and it continues to do so. A newcomer in the field and an interested layperson will undoubtedly find a lot of useful information put in a clear, accessible and concise way by a prominent scholar. With its clarity and precision, this is a text that, in many ways, set the standards for similar and more detailed studies in the years to come.

10. Mesoamerican Dualism

Rudolf van Zantwijk, Rob de Ridder, and Edwin Braakhuis (eds.), *Mesoamerican Dualism/ Dualismo mesoamericano*. Symposium ANT 8 of the 46th International Congress of Americanists, Amsterdam 1988. Utrecht: I.S.O.R., 1990. 190 pp., figs., tabs., illus., map.

This book includes 17 essays that were originally presented at the 1988 International Americanists' Congress in The Netherlands. In a field like Mesoamerican studies where our conceptions and ideas change so rapidly as a result of new discoveries and insights the editors and the publisher should be complimented for putting together this interesting set of papers in a relatively brief time period. On the other hand, the title *Mesoamerican Dualism* could be slightly misleading. Among the essays that are really dedicated to the study of dualism (in the book, chapters nos. 2-12), the vast majority address dualism only in the Valley of Mexico (nos. 4-11), while the first two (nos. 2 and 3) are of a more general nature. Essays number 13 through 18 deal with aspects of ceremonial and ritual life that might include (but are not exclusively focused on) dualism in the Maya area (nos. 13-15), Oaxaca (nos. 17 and 18), and a modern community in Michoacán (no. 16).

The editors begin their Introduction with the statement that "In the entire cultural area we call Mesoamerica, the occurrence of dual or bipartite structures constitutes an elementary fact" (1). This is a very important sentence for the understanding of the general theoretical framework in which this symposium (and, subsequently, this book) has been conceived: a hypothesis (dualism as "an elementary fact") has been set forth as a foundation for other hypotheses. The fact that the basic hypothesis has not been proven is left out of sight. What readers do not know cannot hurt them. The idea is present in the title of Nigel Davies' essay "Dualism as a Universal Concept: Its Relevance to Mesoamerica" (8-14). However, I believe that a much more valid assessment of this idea is given in the contribution by Jacqueline de Durand-Forest and Edouard-Joseph de Durand, "Dualisme et/ou ambivalence dans le panthéon aztèque" (15-20). While delimiting the area of their inquiry, the authors actually go to the sources (in this case, early Colonial documents and manuscripts) in order to check if the concept of dualism as we know it from the Old World (primarily from orphism, gnosticism, and the ancient Iranian religion) can be applied to the Aztec gods. Not surprisingly, the concept of dualism appears to be too narrow and they propose the term "ambivalence." The editors themselves do not agree with this approach (2 ff.).

It seems to me that the editors have failed to clearly explain the theoretical and methodological framework of the book. Dualism does not appear in Mesoamerica before the Late Postclassic and Colonial periods – unless one considers representations of marriage as some kind of a dualism involving male and female. When it is documented, it seems to be heavy influenced by the Spanish missionaries and the need to present native nobility's religious view in a more acceptable way for the conquerors. It is true that this concept might be associated with some Postclassic deities – like Quetzalcoatl. On the other hand, Quetzalcoatl appears in many more than two aspects (Ehecatl, Yoalli Ehecatl, Xolotl, Tlahuizcalpantecuhtli, Nanahuatzin, Tecciztecatl, Nacxit, etc.). Of course, there is always an option to simply ignore some aspects or take them two at a time – but where does it lead?

Another problem is that interpretative and symbolic anthropology are underrepresented in the Mesoamerican studies. Little or no attention has been paid to the role of those interpreting the natives' point of view. Practically no effort has been made to understand the natives' actions in relation to the norms of their cultures before contact, and works like León-Portilla (1959), Clendinnen (1987), Farris (1984) and Jones (1989) still remain widely ignored – despite the well-deserved recognition that they have received in academic circles.

But this is still a very interesting and readable book. The majority of authors have focused on very specific issues, from the discoveries in the Aztec Templo Mayor to the cargo system among the Mixe. Some problems arise with the contributions whose conclusions have been out-dated by subsequent research (like Graulich's very thorough study of the symbolism of the murals in Cacaxtla). Also, De Ridder's essay "Peoples and Places – The Epi-Toltec Immigrants of the Guatemalan Highlands and Their Interrelations" raises some very interesting questions about the widespread interpretations of the K'iche' political structure and the role of lineages. However, de Ridder accepts as "well-known" that "the *Popol Vuh* gives an indigenous view of creation and exodus" (149). It should be noted that the earliest version of this text has been written down in the early 1700s (a century and a half after the conquest of the area) by Spanish missionaries – so how indigenous can this really be (cf. Edmonson 1964, 1978, 1979; Rivera Dorado 2000; Van Akkeren 2003)? The other problem is that the *Popol Vuh* itself is a sacred book of a specific lineage (Kaweq, one of the ruling families in the K'iche' capital at the time of the conquest), so it is unclear how the author wants to employ the idea that "any lineage model" could have "no value for anthropological analysis" (165). The present example certainly demonstrates that the importance of kinship cannot be overstated in interpreting the ancient Highland Maya documents and chronicles. But perhaps this should be left for another book.

11. Forest of Kings

Linda Schele and David Freidel, *A Forest of Kings: The Untold Story of the Ancient Maya*. New York: William Morrow and Company, 1990. 542 pp., figures, maps, colour photographs, glossary, notes, index, bibliography.

Every field of study has its classic works, works considered to be landmarks in the specific field, frequently recalled and cited in the future. *A Forest of Kings* is bound to become a such classic in Maya studies, and in many aspects this book resembles an earlier classic in this field, Sir J. E. S. Thompson's *The Rise and Fall of Maya Civilization*, first published in 1954 (Thompson 1966a). It is beautifully written (for which credit should be given not only to the authors but also to the publisher's professional writer, Joy Parker), it incorporates some of the most recent data available, numerous illustrations and colour photographs (not all of which are by Justin Ker as implied on the frontispiece) are wonderfully incorporated in the text, and this inexpensive volume can serve as an excellent guide to the world of ancient Maya civilization.

The title resembles (and immediately summons to mind) an important work in another field (African studies): Victor Turner's *Forest of Symbols* (Turner 1967). Like Turner before them, Schele and Freidel are primarily concerned with symbolic meanings. To some extent, the ancient Maya did live in forests of symbols, since they called their pyramids "mountains" and the stelae "trees" or "tree-stones." Everything in their world had a different set of meanings, and the authors set out to decode these meanings through the study of ancient Maya symbols and rituals. Maya rituals are viewed from the perspective of their own history (of course, one should bear in mind that what we have are mostly archaeological records about the life of the highest class of the society, which constituted perhaps not more than 1.5 per cent of the total population), and corroborated by interdisciplinary research (Schele came to this field as an a historian, Freidel as an archaeologist). Both authors have conducted some important field research in different sites and in different parts of the Maya area (Freidel at Cozumel island, Cerros and Yaxuná: Schele at Palenque and Copán), and the results of their research form a significant part of the book. There are ten chapters, arranged in more or less chronological order, and dealing with different major Maya centres, from the Preclassic (Cerros), to Early Classic (Tikal and Uaxactún) and Late Classic period (Yaxchilán and Palenque), into the Postclassic (Chichén Itzá). The authors put considerable emphasis on iconography, especially the iconography of royal autosacrifice and war.

While most people interested in this subject will certainly find the amount of data presented fascinating, the fact that this book was primarily written for readers without much (or any) background in ancient Mesoamerican civilizations should always be remembered, especially when reading about the individuals named "Lady Beastie," or some other rather freely transcribed names and titles. In this case, this person was eventually identified as a *male ruler* by David Stuart (Skidmore 2005: 67). For example, translating *Ch'ul Way Ahau* as "Holy Shaman Lord" (141) implies at least two concepts whose exact meaning in the ancient Maya world we simply do not know (*holy* and *shaman*). Furthermore, not many epigraphers would accept translating *way* as "shaman," since the Mayan glyph covers much broader range of meanings (Houston and Stuart 1989: 5).

There are some other minor methodological problems, like the authors' uncritical acceptance of Peter Mathews' work with emblem glyphs to define the Classic Maya polities (58-59). The question of the real meaning and the significance of the emblem glyphs is still open. From recent decipherments by Steve Houston and David Stuart it is really hard to accept the "emblem glyphs" only as political markers – it seems much more likely that they represent spiritual or symbolic domains of certain rulers or ruling families. In fact, the authors are more cautious in the notes (cf. 423-424), and provide more background information. Also, statements like: "The Maya fought not to kill their enemies but to capture them" (143) are remnants of a slightly idealistic and highly unrealistic view concerning war practices in the ancient Mesoamerica (but promoted by Thompson in his classic work). The Maya, like their neighbours, wanted to capture their enemies and the captives of noble rank were highly prized – but they also fought to kill and destroy, just like everyone else. (It is too bad that the manuscript of the book was actually finished by mid-1989, so recent data on the war practices around Dos Pilas and the whole Petexbatún area could not be incorporated.)

Another problem concerns interpreting Palenque texts as "the only full statement of creation mythology and its relationship to the institution of *ahau* (*ajaw*) that we have from the Classic Maya period" (244). There is simply no proof that something like the pan-Maya creation mythology or "pantheon" ever existed (as Knorozov 1964 claimed). Most recent research implies existence of the much more localized clusters of gods connected or associated with rulers, ruling families and specific sites (Estrada Belli 2006). We might find the iconographic traits associated with the gods of the so-called "Palenque Triad" in other locations, but how do we know that their meaning was the same? Especially given the fact that the ancient Maya spoke different languages. Also, the texts found in Palenque are in many ways exceptions – they cannot be taken to imply a model that can be used to interpret inscriptions from other sites (as noted in chapter 5, above).

But even with some objections regarding method and context, this remains a remarkable work that draws heavily upon the most recent decipherments dealing with Classic Maya political history. History in the Maya world was also prophecy, a guide for the future, and a set of codes and regulations. For the first time in more than two decades, a single volume presents us with a rare opportunity to take a look at this wonderful history and how the ancient Maya narrated important events.

FIG. 5. PLASTER PORTRAIT OF QUIRIGUA RULER K'AK' TILIW CHAN YOPAAT (REIGNED 724-785), AFTER STELA C (DEDICATED IN 775), MADE BY ALFRED P. MAUDSLAY (1850-1931) DURING HIS 1880S RESEARCH IN GUATEMALA. MUSEUM OF ARCHAEOLOGY AND ANTHROPOLOGY, UNIVERSITY OF CAMBRIDGE.

12. The Meaning of Maya Myths

Introduction: Method, Context and Interpretation

Each thing was made silent,
Each thing was made calm,
Was made invisible,
Was made to rest in heaven.
(Edmonson 1971: 9-10; lines 125-128.)

Understanding Maya myths is of supreme importance for comprehending their religion and worldview – more precisely, a variety of cults,[13] rituals, and beliefs that form their "part" in Mesoamerican religions. This complex is very specific because of the great number of common beliefs and similar rituals, as well as numerous deities that have common traits in different civilizations – extending from the "Olmec" and Teotihuacán to the Zapotec, Toltec, Mixtec, and Aztec. In this universe of extraordinary cultures the Maya have a very important place.

However, each study of Maya religion is rendered much more difficult by the lack of the sources. The little we know comes mostly from the Postclassic period (10th-16th centuries CE) and the question regarding the extent of continuity between the Classic and Postclassic is still open (see, for example, Edmonson 1979: 157-166). What survived are stelae, lintels, reliefs, bas-reliefs, and figurines and sculptures on one hand – and ceramics and oral tradition on the other, with a few manuscripts written down during the colonial period, of which "Popol Vuh" is the most important for the subject of this paper. The trails of ancient beliefs can be found even in some very "Christian" ceremonies of the present-day Maya. As noted by Thomas Gann (1918: 40): "Nominally, they are Christians, but the longer one lives among them, and the better one gets to know them, the more he realizes that Christianity is to a great extent merely a thin veneer, and that fundamentally their religious conceptions and even their ritual and ceremonies are survivals – degenerate, much changed, and with most of their significance lost – but still survivals of those of their ancestors of pre-Columbian days."

Having in mind all these obstacles, it is no wonder that there are only a few useful studies of Maya religion. However, it is only in the last 50 years that we are witnessing the gradual accumulation of knowledge on different aspects of their society and culture, including religion. If one turns to mythology, a very important break through has been made in the decipherment of most Mayan hieroglyphs (Grube and Gaida 2006), study of ceramics found in the dignitaries' tombs (Adams 1971), and great progress made in the study of art and iconography (Kampen 1981; Baudez 2004) and works that point to the legacy of ancient beliefs in present-day communities (Scholes and Roys 1948). There

---

[13] For the definition of cult which is in my opinion especially valid for the religious complexes of this part of the world, I refer to Brundage (1985: 4 ff.). He stresses that "Failure in it [cult - A.B.] leads to the disorientation of the group and the unpinning of its value systems."

has been a lot of dispute about the methodological approach employed in the study of iconography, which directly influences the study of religion and myths. On the one hand, there is the so-called "direct historical approach," based on the comparative study of Mesoamerican civilizations (predominantly Aztec), as well as on modern ethnological research. This approach has been accepted by many of the leading authorities in Maya studies (like Gordon R. Willey), and I think that its best presentation and defence against its critics has been that of Henry B. Nicholson (1976: 157-175). On the other hand is the intrinsic configurational iconographic analysis proposed by George Kubler (1972), but also supported by scholars like Jiménez Moreno (1971). However, despite the strength of their arguments and the remarkable academic reputation of these two scholars, their attempt to point to some remarkable inconsistencies in interpretations of Mesoamerican religions (including the Maya) was mostly ignored – at least until the 1990s and the large-scale decipherment of Mayan texts and their practical implications (for example, Houston and Stuart 1996).[14] The Mayas were at the same time *familiar* (as they had been critically studied for almost a century by then), and *exotic*, as representatives of the ultimate others, Native Americans. This familiarity translated into attempts to bring them closer to the contemporary public. Observations of beliefs and rituals made during the 20th century about particular ethnographic communities were simply transferred into the past. In this way, *anthropological* data from the present were used to interpret *archaeological* data in the past – until two decades ago, seriously hampered by the inability of most scholars to read Maya script.

As another note on methodology, it should be noted that the "direct historical approach" was first challenged by art historians and iconographers. Contemporary judgments may be made about an ancient work of art, but very few scholars would then take her or his *impression* of that work of art as an integral part of its meaning. For example, no one has attempted to seriously interpret ancient Greek religion by interviewing citizens of contemporary Greece, nor am I aware of the interpretations of ancient Roman religion through interviews of the citizens of present-day Italy. Somehow, however, such an approach has been seen as perfectly legitimate when it comes to establishing connections between contemporary Mayas and their distant ancestors – even when there were no elements that would enable one to determine which ethnic group ancestors belonged to or which language they spoke. The leading Maya art historian of the second half of the 20th century, George Kubler, proposed instead what he called (following Renaissance art historian Erwin Panofsky) an "intrinsic approach" – looking at images in the context where they originated, and trying to interpret them from that very same context.[15]

---

[14] I should add that the epigraphers who were mostly responsible for the breakthrough in the decipherment of ancient Maya script, Houston and Stuart (as well as their students and colleagues), were very well aware that the wild analogies in the interpretations of Maya iconography (that were subsequently "exported" onto their religion and ritual) simply did not work, but their work was considered to be "too specialized" or even "exotic" for the members of the wider Mesoamericanist academic community.

[15] Panofsky insisted on the understanding of the particular imagery (iconology) as the basis of eventual understanding of its meaning in the wider context (iconography): "...the correct identification of motifs is the prerequisite of their correct iconographical analysis, so is the correct analysis of images, stories and allegories the prerequisite of their correct iconological interpretation" (1955: 32).

But the subject of this chapter is the meaning of Maya myths, especially regarding customs and beliefs of other Mesoamerican peoples, and the fact that about some of them we know much more (those from the Valley of Mexico in the first place). I prefer to call this a comparative approach, which does not mean that I take data from other cultures to interpret Maya myths – my only interest is in comparing them, because certain "types" or "models" are encountered in different traditions (which does not mean that they were "carried" or "diffused" from culture to culture), suggesting similar models of the manifestations of the sacred. It will become obvious that in some cases we deal with patterns characteristic of this part of the world, while in others Maya tradition retains a sort of "exclusiveness." I must note that I use the word *myth* to denote *a traditional tale*, one aiming at a symbolic explanation of the world around us and the paradoxical ambiguity of human existence, as well as at the justification of the present hierarchy and social order (among gods or men). We do not deal with some sort of "pre-scientific" or "proto-scientific" thinking. The point is that everything important and fascinating was to be explained through mythic thinking as the adequate sphere of symbolic expression (Kirk 1970; Bošković 2002). It excludes bivalent logic and many other relations familiar to us (before/after; cause/effect; etc.). Myth as symbol offers ground for the development and extension of all human intellectual and creative activity, especially the inclination towards the gathering and classifying of notions and concepts, which enabled mythical heroes to become subject(s) of religious cults. The evidence we have justifies the term "Maya myths" because, despite the regional, language, and cultural differences, there is a corpus of myths common to the majority of Maya groups, as well as to their Mesoamerican neighbours. I shall deal here only with characteristic myths on creation, divine hero-twins, and moon goddess.

1. Ages of the World

> [The day] 4 Ahau will be creation.
> [The day] 4 Ahau will be darkness.
> Then were born the heart of creation,
> the heart of darkness. (Roys 1965: 6)

The myth of the periodic cycle of cosmic destruction and renovation, the so-called "ages of the world" (or suns in Nahuatl tradition), is common to all Mesoamerican cultures and has also parallels among the Indians of the Southwest of the USA. According to the version given by Tozzer (1907: 153-154) - and based on informants from the vicinity of Valladolid - the present world is in its fourth "age." At first, it was inhabited by *zayamuincob* ("the disjointed men"), dwarfs capable of carrying large stones on their hunched backs. This strength and their miraculous ability to bring firewood to the hearth by whistling, enabled them to build ancient cities and huge paved roads. There also existed a great road suspended in the sky, stretching from Tulum and Coba to Chichén Itzá and Uxmal. A great living rope was also connected with this road (blood flowed in the interior of it), and it served as a mean by which gods sent food to the ancient cities' rulers. In the course of time men had become wicked, so gods decided to destroy the world using a flood *hayiokocab* ("water over the earth"). The rope was cut, all the blood flowed out, and it disappeared forever. Until then all was still in darkness.

In the midst of unending gloom the sun suddenly rose for the first time and its rays turned the industrious dwarfs into stone. In the next creation there lived people called *dz'olob*, but they were destroyed by another flood. In the third period, the world was inhabited by *macehualli* (Nahuatl word for "ordinary people"), ancestors of the present-day Mayas. These were destroyed by a *hunyecil* ("hurricane and earthquake") or *bulcabal*. Finally, the present world is inhabited by the descendants of all the ancient races and will disappear after a flood (a fire, according to "Relación de Merida"--but one must remember that, for the ancient Mesoamericans, water and fire were not opposites).

According to the "Popol Vuh," the first people were just "dolls made of wood" – they watched... talked... multiplied... but had no heart or soul, and they were not even aware of their creators – so they had to be destroyed:

> Then their flood was invented by the heart of
> Heaven
> A great flood was made, and descended on the heads
> Of those who were dolls
> Who were carved of wood. (Edmonson 1971: 25-26)

Besides this flood their utensils and domestic animals also rebelled against the first people, and had prominent part in their annihilation. From the few survivors descended monkeys... In the second creation, it seemed that the work of the gods was well executed, since the people were really brilliant:

> They came to see;
> They came to know
> Everything under heaven
> If they could see it.
> (Edmonson 1971: 150)

But the gods were far from being satisfied with their brilliancy:

> "It is not good
> What they said,
> Our forming
> Our shaping:
> We know everything great
> And small," they said.
> And so they took back again
> Their knowledge,
> Did Bearer
> And Engenderer.
> (Edmonson 1971: 151-152)

The first pair of divine hero-twins, 1 Hunter (*Hun Hunahpu*) and 7 Hunter (*Vuqub Hunahpu*), were defeated by the Lords of the Underworld (*Xíbalba*, "place of dread").

This world was also inhabited by giants, led by 7 Parrot (*Vuqub Kaqix*) and his sons Alligator (*Cipacna*) and 2 Leg (*Kaab r Aqan*). They were all killed by the next pair of hero-twins who, afterwards, proceeded to defeat the Lords of the Underworld. Of special interest among all these giants is the story of the Alligator, whose only "sin" seems to have been some sort of *hubris* and who slayed 400 young men – an episode resembling similar adventure of the great Mexica Aztec warrior god Huitzilopochtli (cf. the chapter on Aztec Great Goddesses).

In the third creation a dramatic showdown between the hero-twins and the Lords of the Underworld took place; and finally, in the fourth creation, people were made of yellow and white maize.

According to Mexican tradition, the first creation was 4 Jaguar (*naui ocelotl*)[16] and the world was inhabited by giants. After 13 periods of 52 years these giants were devoured by jaguars. Tezcatlipoca was the sun of this age. The second creation was named 4 Wind (*naui ehecatl*), and Quetzalcoatl was its sun. After 7 periods of 52 years this world was destroyed when terrible winds swept away houses, trees, and people, and survivors were turned into monkeys. The next creation was 4 Rain (*naui quiauitl*) and Tlaloc was its sun. After 6 cycles of 52 years it ended in a rain of fire from the sky and volcanic eruptions. This world was inhabited by children who were afterwards turned into birds. The fourth creation was 4 Water (*naui atl*), its sun being goddess Chalchihuitlicue. After 13 periods of 52 years the world was destroyed by floods and people were turned into fish. Finally, we live in the time of the fifth creation, 4 Movement (*naui ollin*), whose sun is Tonatiuh. People were made of bones brought from the Underworld by Quetzalcoatl and the present world will be destroyed by a series of earthquakes.

This symbolism is quite complex when we bear in mind that, for example, jaguars were believed to represent "des forces obscures de la terre, de tout le mystère qui rôde 'au cœur des montagnes'" (Soustelle 1967: 8). The feline cult is one of the most prominent ritual practices of "Olmec" religion in ancient Mexico, where it can be traced as far back as the 12th century BCE, and it is also characteristic of many pre-Columbian South American cultures (starting with 850 BCE in Chavin, Peru). It seems that many different cultures regarded the jaguar as their ancestor and the continuity of this belief was preserved at the time of the Conquest, since "the jaguar was an important emblem of their [Aztec] all-powerful Smoking Mirror God [Tezcatlipoca]" (Davies 1982: 48). The myths related to the jaguar's role in creation and destruction of the world have numerous variations,[17] but they all reflect basic concepts of these cultures: that the world is periodically being created and destroyed. Here, destroying should not be taken

[16] In this brief account I follow the most widely accepted order, but León-Portilla (1961: 14-17), based on the 16th century manuscript known as "Anales de Cuauhtitlán," presents these ages in a different order: 4 Atl, 4 Ocelotl, 4 Quiauitl, 4 Ehecatl, 4 Ollin.
[17] It is very interesting to compare these traditions with the ones from American Southwest. Hopis believe that they have come to earth, the Fourth world, after passing from three other worlds, and each world is placed in the layer above the former one. A very complex Navaho myth explains how their ancestors reached the Fifth world, the world we live in, using extremely intriguing symbolism (for the Hopi tradition see Harold Courlander (1982); and the Navaho myth is reprinted in Frederick W. Turner (1974).

as a mere destruction; essentially, it represents renovation, the new world is always better than the former one.

The difference in the number of the "ages of the world" in two Mesoamerican traditions – four for the Maya and (usually) five for the people from the Valley of Mexico – appears unusual. But both quantities mark the same basic concept. Postclassic Maya tradition mentions four cosmic trees (*yaxche*) placed at the four world directions – which denote their colour: red at east, white at north, black at west, and yellow at south. This idea unites the image of the "tree of life" (with the treetop belonging to the heaven, trunk to the earth, and roots to the underworld) as the *axis mundi* with numinous "bearers" (which, like Hellenic Atlantes, hold the sky on their shoulders). Such "fusion" of two cosmological concepts has in the course of time caused the change from the belief that the world is "supported" by four trees into the more anthropomorphic belief that it is "supported" by four gods. The Nahuatl myth explains that, when Tezcatlipoca and Quetzalcoatl have destroyed the world with a flood, four men survived – so the gods transform them into the trees and place them at the four corners of the world. The Maya "bearers" were known as Bacabs, and their oldest representation was found at the Temple 22 at Copán, dating from the 8th century CE (Baudez et Becquelin 1984: 384). In his "Relación de las cosas de Yucatan," written in the 16th century Landa described them,

> Among the multitude of gods which this nation worshipped they worshipped four, each of them called Bacab. They said that they were four brothers whom God placed, when he created the world, at the four points of it, holding up the sky so that it should not fall. They also said of these Bacabs that they escaped when the world was destroyed by the deluge (1985: 115; see also Tozzer 1941: 135-136).

By determining four basic points they also determine whether particular years will be generally good or bad for people (Landa witnessed the New Year ceremonies where Bacabs were of great importance) – and that is where the role of priests as "mediators" became very important.

But why number 4? In Mesoamerican iconography this number is associated with the sun (Beyer 1928: 32 ff.) – representing its creative power as "life-giver" and "fire in the sky." When the sun appeared for the first time (13.0.0.0.0. 4 Ajaw 8 Cumku, corresponding to 11 August 3114 BCE in our calendar – the date of the creation of the world),[18] the Maya started their "Long Count" (Spanish *Cuenta larga*). It is quite predictable that the sun, whose daily and nightly journey[19] dominate the great part of Maya religion and which witnesses and participates in all the important events in the sky and in the realm of Xíbalba, determines the ages of the world. And it is quite natural that these ages are called "suns" in the Nahuatl tradition.

---

[18] This particular "age of the world" ended on 21 December 2012.

[19] After sunset it is to become a "Jaguar-Sun," which is led by the young moon goddess towards the place where it will be ritually decapitated; but the female counterpart of the great underworld jaguar – analogous to the Aztec Tepeyollotl ("Heart of the Mountain") – will just before dawn give birth to a new sun, now led by the old moon goddess towards the place where it is supposed to start another day.

The fifth age is a sort of "appendix" derived from the need to "unite" four sides of the world. So beside four sacred trees (*yaxche* – white one in the North, yellow in the South, red in the East, and black in the West), an additional one, blue/green,[20] is placed in the centre (cf. Bricker 1983). Furthermore, the great importance of rain and related divinities throughout Mesoamerica must not be forgotten, since 5 is also a cipher that "symbolizes" rain (Beyer 1928: 36). This recalls the cosmological concepts of North American Indians where, beside four points for the world directions, a fifth one (*pou sto*) is added in the very centre, signifying the observer (Alexander 1920: 52).

Sun symbolism, along with the creation of corn, is connected with many scenes on murals and ceramics, but it is especially interesting if one follows the adventures of the hero-twins preserved in the written documents. The myth of the divine hero-twins is characteristic of many American Indian traditions. They are present in myths and tales as legendary ancestors and heroes that must overcome various trials. The most interesting detail regarding 1 Hunter (*Hunahpu*) and Jaguar-Sun (*Xbalanqué*) is their role in the creation of the world. Edmonson's "Second Creation" obviously places them in the same world as the giants. Their ancestors, the Maize Twins (1 Hunter and 7 Hunter), were defeated in the sacred ball game by the Lords of Xíbalba and ritually decapitated. In retaliation Hunahpu and Xbalanque went on to "avenge" them and (on the cosmic level) to defeat Death.

Their descent metaphorically represents the descent of the sun and, on a broader scale, it serves as an example of the trials the deceased ruler must encounter on his or her journey. However, they will prove to be much wiser and more skilled than their father and uncle (although Hunahpu will, during the night in the house of Killer Bat, also be decapitated, and his brother for some time will replace his head with a squash) and finally defeat the "Lords of the Night," sacrificing two of them, and dispersing the others. After all their exploits,

> (...) they walked back up
> Here amid the light,
> And at once
> They walked into the sky.
> And one is the sun,
> And the other of them is the moon.
> (Edmonson 1971: 144)

A new ritual pattern is established after their victory. Until their descent, the Lords of the Underworld had been absolutely merciless: Death was the supreme ruler and its superiority was confirmed by the sun sacrifice already mentioned above.

Hunahpu and Xbalanque did not abolish the sacrifice, as it was essential for the creation of the world. Thus, Hunahpu will be decapitated – but he will get his head back in a miraculous way. According to Thompson (1950: 87-88), Hunahpu is the K'iche' day

---

[20] Yucatec Maya have the same word (*yax*) for both blue and green.

corresponding to Yucatec 1 *Ajaw*, the day that "belongs" to the sun god. Among the contemporary K'iche' Maya the word *junajpu* also signifies player par excellence). The defeated players in the sacred ball game were also decapitated, an event resulting in the miracle needed for the maize to grow (Baudez 1984). Death and rebirth are suggested with the appearance of hero-twins in the form of men-fish. Furthermore, it seems that many Mesoamerican Indians believed that gods "catch" fish – representing human embryos that float in the mythical lake whose Nahuatl equivalent is Tamoanchán (Dütting 1976: 42-43 ff.). This power of the gods is also suggested by the image of the Bone MT-51:A of Tikal Temple 1, Burial 116, in which three long nosed gods (identified as Chac Xib Chacs) are depicted capturing fish. However, it should not be forgotten that long-nosed heads were also aspects of the primordial alligator. Their association with resurrection is perhaps the most important mark of the victorious divine twins. Their victory was eternalized in the sun's "taking over" of the ball game; and in that extraordinary ambience the sun's underworld journey will be experienced forever.

2. The Maya Moon Goddess and the Mystery of Creation

> Who is your tree? Who is your bush?
> What was your trunk when you were born?
> (Roys 1965: 4)

The above incantation reflects an ancient belief, found even today among the Maya, that a certain animal or plant "watches" the fate of each individual. "Ritual of the Bacabs" shows the healer and medicine man's efforts to determine which plant "guards" the sick one. Such knowledge enables him to cure the plant, too, and to find the exact place where sickness is located. This belief probably results from the ancient fascination with the mystery of life and the imposing veneration of ancestors (deities were ancestors of specific ruling lineages in various Maya city-states). Furthermore, everyone has his "animal spirit companion" – Nahuatl *nahual*. On its underworld journey, the deceased is led by the horrible dog known among the Postclassic Yucatec Maya as Xul – Nahuatl Xolotl, Aztec Xulotl. Or, as summed by Vogt, when writing about a modern Maya community during 1960s:

> Each person and his animal spirit companion (*vay-j-el* or *wayhel* in most Tzotzil communities, but *chanul* in Zinacantán) share the same soul (*ch'ulel* in Tzotzil). Thus, when the ancestral gods install a soul in the embryo of a Zinacanteco, they simultaneously install the same soul in the embryo of an animal. Similarly, the moment a Zinacanteco baby is born a supernatural jaguar, coyote, ocelot, or other animal is born. Throughout life, whatever happens of note to the Zinacanteco happens to the animal spirit companion, and vice versa. (Vogt 1969: 372)

These "animal spirit companions" are kept in some sort of corral by the ancestral deities. The "instalment of the soul" was probably done by an aspect of the Earth Goddess (or what some scholars called "Great Goddess"). Among the Mayas one sees her in at least two important aspects: as young moon goddess (Postclassic Yucatec Ixchel, Goddess I in the codices, according to Schellhas' classification) and also as an old goddess with jaguar claws and spouse of the creator god, who was in Postclassic Yucatan known as Ix Chebel Yax (Goddess O in Schellhas' classification). Both aspects can be recognized among the four goddesses that Landa (1985: 49; Tozzer 1941: 10) mentions as the ones venerated on the island of Cozumel – Ix Chel, Ix Chebel Yax, Ix Hunie, Ix Hunieta. There is some evidence that suggests the latter two are the same deity, and the question about the actual relationship between Ixchel and Ix Chebel Yax is very interesting (cf. Tozzer 1941: notes 46, 47). Thompson (1939) regarded them as the same deity, but later (1970) changed his mind. It seems that Landa considered them to be mother and daughter, as did Knorozov (1964: 3). However, if one accepts the general notion that Maya and Mesoamerican deities more generally presented themselves in different aspects, these two could be treated as one deity[21]. Ixchel is also being mentioned as a goddess of childbirth and medicine in Landa's manuscript, while Scholes and Roys (1948: 57) give more information in their excellent monograph,

> Ix Chel was evidently a very popular deity among the Chontal generally. Her shrine on Cozumel Island off the northeastern coast of Yucatan was visited by pilgrims from Tabasco, and the site of Tixchel, which was twice occupied by Acalan, [and] was apparently named for her. As Seler pointed out, the names of Ciuatecpan ("palace of the woman") on the Usumacinta and of Ciuatan ("the place of the woman") in central Tabasco must refer to her worship. Landa notes that Isla de Mujeres ("island of the women") north of Cozumel was named for the idols of goddesses which were found there. He names Ix Chel and three others, but Tozzer suggests that at least two of them were the same deity. In Tabasco on the Rio Chico, a branch of the Usumacinta, is a site named Cuyo de las Damas, which may well refer to Ix Chel also. She was probably the goddess to whom, according to Cortés, the people of Teutiercas in Acalan dedicated their principal temple. In her "they had much faith and hope." In her honor "they sacrificed only maidens who were virgins and very beautiful; and if they were not such, she became very angry with them." For this reason they took especial pains to find girls with whom she would be satisfied and brought them up from childhood for this purpose.

While the reliability of Cortes' account can be doubted, this sort of sacrifice is similar to the one that the Aztecs had in the month Ochpaniztli, especially that in benefit of *ixiptla* (impersonator) of the goddess Chicomecóatl ("Seven Snake") (Brundage 1985: 51-54), although they made sacrifices to the four aspects of their Great Goddesses. Toci ("Grandmother") is the most interesting of these, since her equivalent among the Yucatec Maya is Ix Chebel Yax. Originally the Great Goddess (and the moon goddess, too) of the Huastecs, she was "via Culhuacán" absorbed into the Aztec pantheon (Brundage 1985: 51). As an old goddess, she reminds one of the image of the Ix Chebel Yax on the page 74 of the *Dresden Codex* (one of the three existing Postclassic Maya codices), but it is also worth noting that weaving and embroidering, which are attributed to Ixchel, are supervised by (and actually are emblems of) Ix Chebel Yax. Her connection with the spindle associates her with the spider (Thompson 1939: 147-149). In the *Dresden Codex* her role as the goddess of fate is emphasized with the prefix *sak*. This prefix means

---

[21] For the detailed treatment of the attributes of merchant gods see Thompson (1966).

(among other things) white, chastity, and virginity – and all of these qualities are also connected with the name of the young moon goddess as White Ix Chel (Roys 1965: 154).

Ixchel was also known as "The One that Emerges from the Sand" and, taking into account the Nahuatl sacrifice of *the* ixiptla of goddess Xilonen, for whom "it was said 'she enters the sand' because in this way she made known her death – that on the morrow she would die" (Dibble 1980: 199), this could express her superiority over death. This could also explain her role in bringing the sun to the underworld altar. She was also considered as an ancestress of the ruling dynasties in several Maya cities, and her power was symbolically given to the ruler in the form of a "bundle of power." On page 18 of the *Dresden Codex* she is depicted both in her terrifying aspects (carrying a skeleton, middle row), as well as the nurturing ones (carrying corn that will be planted, lower row) – in charge of the wellbeing of the whole community.

3. Résumé: The Character of Maya Deities

He is both male and female, and it is the union of this pair which brings about the birth, or sprouting, of the cultivated plants, which are said to be their offspring. (...) *Ihp'en*, as the passive spirit of maize, is said to be a single being and of male sex only. In this role he is the male consort of the female spirit of the beans, *ixq'anan* (Wisdom 1940: 402).

The concept of a fantastic mythical being that in itself unites the fundamental opposites of earth/sky, life/death, male/female, etc., is characteristic of a number of religions, and there is no reason to consider the Maya as an exception. It seems that this mythical being is also present in Mesoamerican beliefs and rituals (as what archaeologists call "Earth Monster," or "Bicephallic Monster" – see Fig. 6), encountered in the sculptures dated around 1000 BCE and associated with earth (Miller and Taube 1993: 126). This symbolic uniting of opposites was sometimes expressed in the idea of a dual ancestor deity (like the already mentioned Central Mexican Ometeotl) or the pair of creator gods (like the Mixtec 1 Flower and 13 Flower). Traces of this relatively late concept can still be seen in the notion of "mother-fathers" in contemporary K'iche' communities. The fantastic mythological being is also considered as a "supporter" of the universe and was designated as Itzamná in Late Postclassic Maya rituals. Although some of his statements are no longer valid (like the one that "Itzam Na was primarily god of the hierarchy" [Thompson 1970: 210]), Thompson (1970: 209-233) has pointed to its many different aspects. The famous representations from Copán (Altar D), Palenque (House E), and Piedras Negras (Stela 25) were also designated as Terrestrial, Bicephallic, and Celestial Monster, respectively. All of these manifestations are nicely summed up by Clemency Coggins (1985: 53-54),

As the reptilian structure of the universe, Itzamná encompasses phenomena that transcended and are antithetical to the sun. It does, however, have distinct celestial and Underworld components like the sun. (...) Supernatural beings often emerge from the open jaws of the celestial serpent and its [serpent's – A. B.] body may consist of a Sky Band, a sequence of celestial signs. This serpent is also commonly represented as the "serpent bar" carried by many Maya lords in their official portraiture, showing that the lord and his lineage worship and many [lords – A. B.] descend from Itzamná. Beneath the human realm, Itzamná symbolized the structure of the earth, and in the waters of the earth and Underworld, where death reigns, it takes the skeletal forms of such aquatic reptiles as crocodiles. These are usually portrayed as Long Nose Heads, either skeletal or with no lower jaw (which means the same thing).

But it is not only Itzamná that embodies binary opposition, as many Maya deities are found in pairs (Maize Twins, hero-twins, the Paddlers from the Underworld, Hun Chuen and Hun Batz, etc.). And such twinned figures are quite common in Native American traditions as well. With respect to Itzamná, it is also worth pointing that Baudez and Becquelin (1984: 394-396) consider only Bicephallic and Celestial Monster, while in a later study of Maya religion Claude Baudez (Baudez 2002), unlike the leading expert in ancient Maya religion, Mercedes de la Garza (2007; de la Garza and and Nájera Coronado 2002), rejects the very existence of this deity.

On a more abstract level of the history of religions there are opposites of light/creation on the one side and darkness/death on the other. The first is a principle connected with sky and male, the other with earth and female. In the "Ritual of the Bacabs" edited by Ralph L. Roys (1965), their union is designated with the word *al* ("birth"). The diurnal Akbal (in other dialects also: Akabal, Uotan, Watan) represents night, the interior of the earth, caves (Thompson 1950: 73-75), but also the jaguar (God L according to Schellhas' classification) as Lord of the Night. According to Tzeltal Maya belief, the same day (*Uotan*) represents the name of their ancestor, who came probably from the east, distributed land among the people, and introduced the art of hieroglyphic writing – the same deeds attributed to Itzamná. Moreover, according to Thompson (1950: 73-75), earlier authorities (Brinton, Seler) supposed that Uotan was a deity analogous to the "Heart of the Sky" from the "Popol Vuh." This set of meanings is derived mostly from 16th century sources and has many parallels with the myths of the Quetzalcoatl. In this specific mythic history ancient gods (obviously belonging to the variety of biologically impossible supernatural beings) are being "transformed" in "culture heroes" and their primary associations are obscured in the past.

In parallel to this dualism and its manifestations, it seems that one can actually talk of several basic groups of relevant mythological material. The "Popol Vuh" complex forms only one part of it (both temporally and geographically limited to the Late Postclassic highland Guatemala). Although parallels might look appealing, one must bear in mind the date and the circumstances of its recording (Edmonson 1971, 1978; Rivera Dorado 1991, 2000; Van Akkeren 2003). Different animals had different meanings in mythical stories. For example, let us consider the frog, which appears in some scenes on ceramics. But the frog is also known as "Uinal Monster," patron of the month (*uinal*). In Edmonson's edition of the "Chilam Balam of Chumayel" there is a beautiful version of a myth named "The Birth of the Uinal." On the conceptual/ symbolic plane, this story also presents the birth of humankind (Edmonson 1986: 30-31; 120-126). It is interesting to note that it is the woman that comes first, and I propose that here we encounter the Postclassic Maya goddess of birth, Goddess I or Ixchel, as she was known in the 16th century Yucatan.

However, we know almost nothing of the majority of episodes depicted on ceramics from the Classic period and earlier (especially vases from private collections, as mentioned in the Preface to this book). The interpretations that considered everything as some episode from the "Popol Vuh" do not lead very far and, helped by the great progress made in the decipherment of Maya hieroglyphs, as well as some impressive new archaeological discoveries, the number of scholars attempting other approaches is increasing,. As already mentioned above, we need sources. Even in their absence we can speculate that there must have been another corpus of myths. Since the Maya believed that in some sense everything was divine (including rivers, trees, stones, etc.) and had to be treated in a way that would ensure manifestation of only the benevolent side of the object or thing, there were probably tales about the encounters of young men with different "sacred" things and of the wanderings of men and women far from home, etc. We can only hope that further work will disclose data regarding this other corpus.

The lack of a hierarchy among Maya deities, or even of a "pantheon" is quite important. There is no doubt that the roles of some were considered to be of special relevance for specific activities Besides the those noted above, we can also note that the Jester God during the Classic period [300-900 CE] is always associated with the ruler and Xtabai during the Postclassic [after 1000 CE] is associated with hunting, for example. Although essentially ambivalent, deities could belong both to the Underworld and the Overworld (as designated by "mirror" signs on their bodies). Some were associated with particular sites (the most famous examples of the Classic period are the Palenque Triad and Water-Lily Jaguar at Tikal), where they were represented more often and possibly were (especially those in animal forms) venerated as ancestors of the ruling dynasties. Only very few were represented in the human form, and although humans occasionally wore masks of the particular deities (e.g., the famous vase from Tomb 116, Tikal), the difference was always made clear.

Whether Maya deities were actually "organized" into different "complexes" (as seem to be the case with the Aztecs) remains unknown. We also do not know the extent to which they accepted deities and cults from other Mesoamerican cultures. In some cases they apparently did. Deities from Teotihuacán appear in places like Tikal during the Classic period, and the Toltec/Mexican Quetzalcoatl appears in Chichén Itzá during the Postclassic. Nevertheless, since there was never a strong, united state among the Maya, the "incorporation" of "foreign" deities for political/ ideological reasons would seem to be unnecessary.

These are only some of the characteristics of Maya deities; the choice is arbitrary and there is still much more to say and explore. And I do hope that the difficulties in this "part" of the Mesoamerican studies will be considered as a challenge and (why not?) as an invitation.

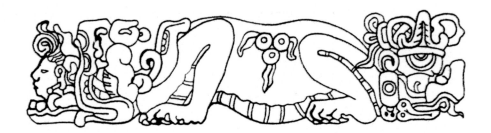

FIG. 6. BICEPHALLIC MONSTER. COPÁN, TEMPLE D, 790. DRAWING BY LIDIJA TARANOVIĆ

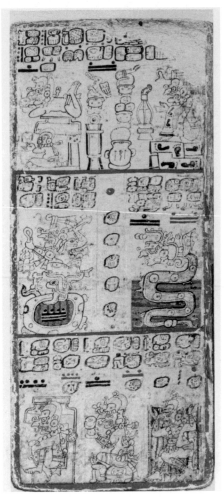

FIG. 7. MAYA MOON GODDESS WITH VARIOUS DEITIES. POSTCLASSIC, DRESDEN CODEX, PAGE 18. AFTER CHROMOLITHOGRAPHIC EDITION BY ERNST FÖRSTEMANN, 1880/1896.

FIG. 8. REPRESENTATIONS OF ITZAMNA FROM THE DRESDEN CODEX, PAGE 35. AFTER CHROMOLITHOGRAPHIC EDITION BY ERNST FÖRSTEMANN, 1880/1896.

13. Interpreting Tlaloc

Rubén Bonifaz Nuño, *Imagen de Tlaloc. Hipótesis iconográfica y textual.*
México: Universidad Nacional Autónoma de México, 1986. 187 pp., fig.
(Estudios de arte y estética, 27.)

For at least 3000 years before the coming of the *conquistadores* Mexico was the scene of a fascinating variety of cultures and societies. Cultures supplanted one another, empires crashed like giants with clay feet, and new ones rose from the obscurity, but they all shared some universal codes of expression, primarily in religion and art. Centuries after the last great empire of the New World had been destroyed, the legacy of these codes still challenges scholars. It is also this legacy that is the core of the work of Rubén Bonifaz Nuño, a Mexican poet whose interesting book on the art of the Aztec Great Temple appeared in 1981, as a result of the research sponsored by the John Simon Guggenheim Memorial Foundation.

Great masterpieces of ancient Mexican art are examined in full detail, with a particular emphasis on something that might be called the „creative human principle." It was creative on behalf of the cultures and peoples of past civilizations. After carefully summing up everything significant that was noted by scholars in the last two centuries, the author discovers in the well-known representations of Tlaloc and Coatlicue the creation of the world as described in the myths, as well as the creative forces. In the case of the colossal statue of Coatlicue from the Museo Nacional de Antropología, these forces are two serpents (according to the myth, disguise taken by Quetzalcoatl and Tezcatlipoca) that enter the body of the great Earth/Mother Goddess (the moment recorded in the sculpture) and eventually split her in two in order to create earth and sky.

The presentation of different opinions and the variety of illustrations make the author's position clear even if one could raise some objections. There are some methodological inconsistencies; Nuño chooses to avoid the written sources (codices) of the colonial period because he doubts their accuracy – but nevertheless relies on later authorities that drew upon these sources, and he uses such a source ("Histoyre de Mexique") himself, when it supports his view. When discussing the Teotihuacán "Tlalocs" there is no mention of what Karl Taube identified as Teotihuacán Spider Woman – and if that is because he disagrees with this identification, it would have been good to give reasons for it.

Although the quest for the ultimate meaning of the images of the two serpents and the human figures is generally much more convincing when focusing on the works of art from the Aztec period (14th-16th centuries CE), this remains a very important and passionately written study. And it is hard to imagine any serious student of Mesoamerican art, iconography, or religion working without consulting it.

14. Templo Mayor

Elizabeth Hill Boone (ed.), *The Aztec Templo Mayor. A Symposium at Dumbarton Oaks, 8th and 9th October, 1983.* Washington: Dumbarton Oaks Research Library and Collection, 1987. 513 pp., fig., maps.

The present volume is the result of a well-prepared symposium that brought together almost all the leading scholars in contemporary Aztec studies. Their meeting was held after the completion of the excavations in the capital of Mexico (*Proyecto Templo Mayor*), begun after the chance discovery of an impressive relief of the dismembered moon goddess Coyolxauhqui on Feb. 21, 1978, and completed in 1982. The full splendour of Mexican Aztec civilization erupted before the eyes of the scholars (and to the public that attended exhibition displays, too), and Aztec studies received a powerful impetus. For years it almost seemed that we knew everything about these people, and in fact, their culture is the best documented of all the cultures in pre-Columbian America. The expectation that "there was not much left to say" had been strengthened after a series of excellent critical editions of first-hand accounts (such as Durán 1867 and Sahagún 1999), and the brilliant works produced in the recent decades, by scholars like Caso (1967), Garibay (1971), Jiménez Moreno (1941), León-Portilla (1959, 1971), Soustelle (1955, 1979), and many others. However, because Aztec art and architecture had rarely been studied within its actual context (in the place where it was meant to be) together with an understanding of its ritual, cosmological, political, and aesthetic significance, there was, indeed, much more.

Some 6000 objects were found during the first phase of the excavations of the main (or great) temple of the Mexican Aztec ritual precinct. Apart from monumental sculptures and their fragments, the great majority of the items consists of offerings, some of which are the subject of the papers by Doris Heyden, Juan Alberto Román Berrelleza, Carlos Javier González González (the latter two being participants of the *Proyecto*), Frances F. Berdan ("The Economics of Aztec Luxury Trade and Tribute"), Johanna Broda, Alfredo López Austin, and Emily Umberger. The two introductory contributions by Elizabeth Hill Boone ("Templo Mayor Research, 1521-1978") and Miguel León-Portilla ("The Ethnohistorical Record for the Huey Teocalli of Tenochtitlan") provide a broad overview, while Eduardo Matos Moctezuma (director of the *Proyecto*) concerns himself in his essay with the general symbolism of the Great Temple. The works of Cecelia F. Klein ("The Ideology of Autosacrifice at the Templo Mayor") and Richard F. Townsend ("Coronation at Tenochtitlan") are among those that will be of great interest, especially for the students of the Mesoamerican iconography. An overall perspective is offered by Esther Pasztory, Henry B. Nicholson, and George Kubler who pose questions and (perhaps most valuably) suggest methodological approaches for further study. Authors of these concluding chapters disagree on certain points (some, like González just list potential problems – without offering solutions). But this dialogue actually enriches the volume as a whole.

The Main Temple was at the centre of Aztec religious life. By extension, it also represented the centre of the empire, of the world, and of the whole universe. The principal responsibility for the maintenance of the universe was in the hands of the priests and officials performing the ceremonies. Ceremonies and rituals ensured that the sacredness of the centre (as *axis mundi*) and of the Mexica Aztecs themselves (as "People of the Sun," as Alfonso Caso famously called them) would continue. By destroying it, the *conquistadores* were able to proceed with the political, cultural, and also the psychical and emotional conquest of Mexico as well. But the traces remained and after more than four centuries they have again been brought to light.

This book stands as a true landmark in Aztec studies, and its scholarly contributions are valuable for the further light they shed on the extraordinary center of Aztec life.

FIG. 9. COYOLXAUHQUI, TEMPLO MAYOR. (AFTER BOŠKOVIĆ 2006.)

15. Aztec Great Goddesses: Their Functions and Meaning

One of the most characteristic features of the Aztec pantheon is the "arrangement" of deities into different complexes: one deity could at the same time be included in various ones. Part of the reason for the amazement on the recognition of this feature was due to the lack of familiarity students of ancient Mexican religions had with other (non-Amerindian) religious traditions. Many of these include different manifestations of the sacred. Especially intriguing is the so-called *Earth-Mother Goddess* complex, in which Nicholson (1971) has included 21 goddesses.

Interest centering on the important female deities has increased after the dramatic discovery of the representation of dismembered Coyolxauhqui on Feb. 21, 1978 (Fig. 9). This magnificent piece (with a diameter varying from 2.95 to 3.25 m, a thickness of 30 to 35 cm, and a maximum height of relief of 10 cm) shows the body of the moon goddess after she was slain by Huitzilopochtli:

> Luego con ella hirió a Coyolxauhqui,
> le cortó la cabeza,
> la cual vino a quedar abandonada
> en la ladera de Coatépetl,
> montaña de la serpiente.
> El cuerpo de Coyolxauhqui
> fue rodando hacia abajo,
> cayó hecho pedazos
> por diversas partes cayeron sus manos,
> sus piernas, su cuerpo.
> (*Códice Florentino,* Lib. III, Cap. I, León-Portilla 1963;
> reprinted in Matos and Ehrenberg 1979: 6)

The dismemberment of deities is present in many mythic or religious traditions. It may have a cosmological (Ymir in Nordic mythology; Puruṣa in Hindu) or ritual function (Sati in Hindu mythology; Osiris in Egyptian), but it is not clear how one should interpret the slaying of this Aztec goddess. Different functions and "readings" of the myth have been suggested. While some authors, such as León-Portilla (1987) and Hultkrantz (1979), suggest that she was slain accidentally (in the course of heading to warn Huitzilopochtli), others, like Carrasco (1987b), "read" the event as it was written down and present her as an inspirer and leader of 400 southerners, who were coming to attack their brother, Huitzilopochtli. A cosmological interpretation has been suggested due to her transformation into the moon while her brothers become the Pleiades, especially considering Huitzilopochtli as a sun god (cf. Soustelle 1940: 8-9). But her slaying might have had a purely ritual function. A two-headed serpent around Coyolxauhqui's waist is tied into a knot and there are also serpents tied in this way around her arms and legs. We know from other Mesoamerican traditions that knots were used as "marks" of the sacrificial victims. Is it possible that the great México Aztec warrior god did not kill his sister but rather offered her as a sacrifice?[22]

Other deities that belong to this complex and were venerated in the time of Aztec supremacy also give rise to some interesting questions regarding their interpretation. Ochpaniztli was the Aztec month in which ceremonies were held in honour of the four aspects of the Great Goddess: Cihuateotl ("the Goddess"), Atlantonan ("Our Mother of Atlan"), Chicomecoatl ("Seven Snake"), and Toci ("Grandmother").

> The first was the latrian form of that bevy of sinister female spirits called the "goddesses" (Cihuateteo). The second was Magna Mother as she patronized certain diseases and maimings and who was additionally connected with water. The third was the Aztec Ceres, the provider of fruits and grains from the earth, particularly maize. The last was a grandly inclusive goddess, the mother of gods, a war goddess, a corn goddess, maker of earthquakes, and patroness of sweatbaths and curing (Brundage 1985: 51).

Rituals connected with this month have already been described in full detail, and I do not intend to repeat these descriptions. However, it should be noted that all activities were divided according to the goddesses' specific functions. For example, the *ixiptla of* Toci (who was an "import" deity, the Aztec version of the great Huastec mother Tlazolteotl) was forced to spin cotton – and spinning and weaving are important attributes of the moon goddesses in a variety of traditions (in fact, Tlazolteotl was the moon goddess). Among the "warrior aspects," the most famous representation is the 2.57 m high sculpture of Coatlicue ("Serpent skirt") at the Mexican Museo Nacional de Antropología. She is portrayed as the bare breasted mother of gods, all arrayed with snakes, severed serpent heads, and human hands and hearts, skulls ... Her hands and feet end in claws because she feeds on corpses. Thus she is "diosa de la tierra, del nacimiento y de la vejez, misterio del origen y del fin, antigüedad y feminidad" (Justino Fernández in León-Portilla 1971: 575). While we have no information on who might have been the father of Coyolxauhqui and her 400 brothers, Huitzilopochtli was conceived in a miraculous way. Coatlicue immediately became pregnant with him when, while sweeping on the sacred mountain Coatepec, a ball of feathers fell from the sky and she pressed it to her breast.

This strange event resembles the Feathered Serpent or Quetzalcoatl, the great Toltec deity and ancestor of their ruling dynasty. According to the hymn that was sung during the Aztec festival Atamalcualiztli (Brundage 1985: 32 ff.), Quetzalcoatl in his fierce aspect as dog-headed Xolotl, carries the corn goddess Xochiquetzal into the underworld and rapes her, after which she gives birth to the young maize god Centeotl. Another myth (León-Portilla 1971: 475 ff.) speaks of Quetzalcoatl's descent into the

---

[22] Although many authors regard the so-called "direct historical approach" as a license to mix data from various Mesoamerican cultures whenever advantageous, I do not advocate such use of cultural materials. In this case, however, the figure itself requires a little bit broader context of possible explanation. For the problems of interpretation, see Matos and Ehrenberg (1979: 70), while for the interpretations of Aztec sacrifice I refer to Anawalt (1982).

underworld to bring the ancestors' bones to be melted by the earth goddess Cihuateotl ("Snake Woman") and sprinkled with blood from his penis. The resulting alloy gives rise to mankind. There is also a legend of Quetzalcoatl (when ruler of Tollan) as son of the hunting god Mixcoatl ("Cloud Snake") and yet another earth goddess, Chimalma. In the version of the myth reported by Thompson (1933: 162), creation of humans is Xolotl's task.

It is obvious from all this that the relationships of this god with the vast number of earth goddesses are extremely complex. It seems that in the period preceding the Conquest these goddesses were responsible for certain "amalgamatic" concepts that were supposed to unite different beliefs belonging to different traditions. The Teotihuacán Feathered Serpent, Toltec Topiltzin Quetzalcoatl, and Aztec Quetzalcoatl are not the same god, although all may have some traits in common. But for the Aztec priests it was necessary to legitimate their people as the logical successor and inheritor of former cultures. The ball of feathers falling from the sky and impregnating Coatlicue was just one of the ways to fulfil this task.

Finally, a note should be added about the principle of duality that was so characteristic of Mexican religion, that is briefly expressed in the following lines from vol. VIII, fol. 175 of the *Textos de Informantes Indígenas* (León-Portilla 1971: 485):

> Y sabían los toltecas
> que muchos son los cielos,
> decían que son doce divisiones superpuestas.
> Allá vive el verdadero dios y su comparte.
> El dios celestial se llama Señor de la dualidad, Ometecuhtli,
> y su comparte se llama Señora de la dualidad, Omecíhuatl, Señora celeste;
> quiere decir:
> sobre los doce cielos es rey, es señor.

This dual deity was also known as Ometeotl, which Davíd Carrasco (in Hinnels 1984: 241) considers as "the fundamental divine power in central Mesoamerican religion." The male "part" of this Supreme God was identified with the sun, the female one with the earth. As Tonacatecuhtli and Tonacacihuatl they were regarded, as respectively, "Lord" and "Lady of Our Flesh." There has been a lot of dispute about the actual antiquity of this concept, since it is exclusively found in Postclassic cultures,[23] but it seems that it has grown out from the need to systematize the "state cults," or, as summed by Davies (1982: 221), the "religion of the priests."

---

[23] Soustelle (in Poupard 1993: 1243) considers this concept to be much older among the Otomi, where it is represented by Otontecuhtli and Tzináná.

Fig. 10. Page 19 of the Codex Borgia. The top of the page shows Tezcatlipoca as the warrior god, while the lower one shows Quetzalcoatl as wind god, Ehecatl.

16. Jacques Soustelle's Studies of Aztec Religion

1. Introduction

The history of the study of ancient Mesoamerican civilizations has always been marked by the presence of exceptional scholars. Along with their research they have included materials related to methodological problems and their personal views and opinions. Thus every single contribution is by itself and within itself also a history of the time period during which the research was conducted.

The work of the great French ethnologist Jacques Soustelle (1912-1990) also can be approached in this fashion, but his work should also be put in a broader context. By the end of the 19th and the beginning of the 20th century, the German scholar Eduard Seler (1849-1922) was already conducting extensive research related to the ancient cultures of Pre-Columbian Mexico. Two magnificent volumes by the Norwegian doctor and explorer Carl Lumholtz (1851-1922) on the ethnography of northern Mexico were published in 1902 and 1903. Initial archaeological excavations were conducted in the Valley of Mexico by Mexican archaeologists, beginning with Leopoldo Batrés, and, in the 1920s, Manuel Gamio (always way ahead of his time) was publishing his magnum opus, the multi-volume *Población del valle de Teotihuacán*. The political aspects of *indigenismo* in Mexican administration lent support for the publication of numerous ethnohistorical sources from the Colonial period. The movement did not last very long, but it permanently influenced people like Angel Ma. Garibay K., Alfonso Caso, Ignacio Bernal, Pedro Armillas, and a little bit later, Miguel León-Portilla. In France, meetings of the Société des Americanistes have grown into the International Congress of Americanists, and the Society's publication, *Journal de la Société des Americanistes*, has become one of the leading publications in the field. The ethnology of ancient Mexico was dominated by eminent scholars like Paul Rivet.

In the early 1930s Soustelle's research was oriented primarily towards ethnology and linguistics, profoundly influenced by his already solid academic background (at the age of 20 he became a professor of philosophy). From 1932 to 1934 he spent most of his time in the field and this research resulted in the monumental work on the Otomi of central Mexico, an essay on the Lacandons of Chiapas, and a lecture "Mexique, terre indienne." This lecture was given in conjunction with an exhibition in the Ethnographical Museum in Paris. The exhibition captured the attention of his colleague, Claude Lévi-Strauss, four years his senior, and permanently diverted his focus to Latin (esp. South) America.

Along with Paul Rivet, Soustelle became one of the founders of the new Musée de l'Homme, where he became co-director. In 1939, he gave a lecture sponsored by the Collège de France (Chaire d'Antiquités américaines, Fondation Loubat), "La pensée cosmologique des anciens Mexicains (Représentation du monde et de l'espace)," which was published a year later (Soustelle 1940).

During World War II he was actively engaged in General de Gaulle's Résistance. In 1945 he became minister of information and afterwards minister of the colonies in the French government. While his political and military engagement is testimony to his enormous energy and the need to speak his mind, it constituted only a short break in his scholarly career. What may may be still the most influential single-volume book on the Aztecs, *La vie quotidienne des Aztèques à la veille de la conquête espagnole* (Daily life of Aztecs on the eve of the Spanish Conquest) was published in 1955. Various articles on certain aspects of the Aztec religion appeared in 1953 (Respect aux dieux morts), 1961 (L'Etat mexicain et la religion), 1966 (Dieux terrestres et dieux célestes dans l'antiquité mexicaine), and 1974 (Aztec Religion). *La pensée cosmologique (...)* and all these articles were published in 1979 in the single volume, *L'Univers des Aztèques*. He also wrote for the *Encyclopaedia Britannica*. Naturally, Soustelle was in charge of the entries on Mesoamerican religions in the *Dictionnaire des religions* under the direction of Cardinal Paul Poupard, whose first edition was published in 1984.

Even from this brief introduction, it is obvious that studies dealing with the Aztec religion form a significant part of Soustelle's work. That is why I will concentrate only on this part, ignoring his linguistic contribution, works on the art in the 1960s, and later volumes on the Olmec (1979a) and Maya (1982).

2. The Role and Function of Religion

For Soustelle, religion primarily has to do with cosmology. Both the structure and the title of his first major ethnographic work support this view. *La pensée cosmologique...* begins with the description of the birth of the present world according to the Colonial period manuscript, "Historia de los Mexicanos por sus pinturas." This is followed by the myth of the four suns of the Aztec world recorded in another Colonial period text, "Anales de Cuauhtitlán." Then comes a brief description of the several important deities (Quetzalcóatl, Cihuateteo, Huehueteotl, Tlaloc), as well as the myth of birth of the Mexica Aztec tribal god, Huitzilopochtli. There are a lot of etymology and ritual-influenced explanations involved, as shown in the following paragraph,

> Le sort normal d'un guerrier, c'est d'offrir des victimes aux dieux, puis de tomber lui-même sur la pierre à sacrifices. Il devient alors, dans les cieux, un compagnon de soleil: Sahagun écrivait, sous la dictée de ses informateurs indigènes: "Le coeur du prisonnier, ils l'appellent précieuse (*tuna*) de l'aigle (*quauhnochtli*). Ils l'élèvent vers le soleil, prince de turquoise (c'est-à-dire: de feu), aigle qui monte; ils le lui offrent, ils l'en alimentent. Et, après l'offrande, ils le placent dans la calebasse de l'aigle (*quauhxicalli*): et, les prisonniers sacrifiés, ils les appellent les gens de l'aigle." Devenus compagnons de soleil, les guerriers sacrifiés le suivent dans la première moitié de sa course, depuis l'Est jusqu'au Zénith, chantant et agitant leurs armes. Au bout de quatre ans, ils se transforment en oiseux-mouches, et reviennent sur la terre. On comprend, dès lors, pourquoi Uitzilopochtli, "l'oiseau-mouche de la gauche", c'est-à-dire du Sud, est à la fois un dieu solaire et la divinité guerrière par excellence (Soustelle 1979b: 101-102).

A significant part of his work is also dedicated to the representations of days and colors, as well as the symbolism connected with the specific cardinal points. Emphasis on time and space as the two fundamental dimensions that delimit human creative and symbolic activity is also present. It is interesting to note that there are also a great deal of comparisons, both within Mesoamerica and cross-culturally. In the table of colors and cardinal points examples are taken from the Maya from Yucatan, Zuni, Tewa, China, and Aztecs. This passion for comparisons will much later lead Soustelle to postulate the existence of the Aztec goddess Chalchihuitlicue on the Relief 1 from Chalcatzingo, 2000 years before the rise of the Aztec state (1979a: 183). (Of course, subsequent studies showed that both the comparison and the gender of the person depicted turned out to be wrong [Grove 1999].)

Both in his most famous work, *La vie quotidienne des Aztèques* (see Chapter III, especially part "Une religion impériale" [1955: 189-194]) and in the articles written during the 1960s (especially "L'Etat mexicain et la religion" [1979b: 21-36]), there is a considerable emphasis on the social component of religion. Religion is always perceived as something within the society itself, and something that influences that society in a variety of ways.

This is connected with the philosophical concept of the human being as a practical being whose symbolic activity changes and remodels the world around him/her. We are what we do?[24] Since living in the community is a characteristic of all human beings, it is necessary to further understand the relationship between religion and society. For Durkheim (1912), religion is an extensive symbolic system that enables social life by expressing and maintaining the social feelings or sentiments and values. Lessa and Vogt (1979) go a little bit further when they perceive the explanation and the expression of ultimate values of society as the primary function of religion. For Durkheim, the ultimate function of religion and its "collective representations" is the establishment of social solidarity among members of the community, in such a way that, in some sense, by worshipping the deities society worships itself. It is not a mere coincidence that one finds numerous references to Durkheim in Soustelle's writings. It is only through understanding the society itself that we can understand Aztec religion. Or, as put at the beginning of his article for the *Encyclopaedia Britannica*: "La religion aztèque est constituée par la mythologie, les croyances et les pratiques du peuple de l'empire aztèque du Mexique pré-cortésien" (Soustelle 1979b: 37).

3. The Principle(s) of Duality

In light of the above disussion, it is not difficult to conclude that Soustelle does not give a definition of the Aztec religion. He is much more interested in its function within the society, in the rituals connected with cults[25] of the various deities, and the human effort to systematize the whole world of symbols that surrounds her/him.

---

[24] And it is easier to understand why Soustelle always insisted on living according to one's own principles – even if it meant spending years in an exile between 1961 and 1968 (for further biographic references, see Duverger 1991). His beliefs are incorporated in the collection of essays on the ancient Mexico (Soustelle 1967).

[25] I use the word "ritual" for actions that, performed in the right way, ensure the harmonious functioning of the family or a group of people. After it is performed for the first time the purpose of the ritual is in its eternal

On the cover of *L'Univers des Aztèques*, there is a scene from the *Codex Borbonicus* (p. 22 of the manuscript), showing Quetzalcóatl in a ritual dance with Tezcatlipoca. Nowotny's comment in Codex Borbonicus (1974: 18-19) is also very instructive for interpreting this scene. According to the 16th century manuscript (*Histoyre de Mexique*), these two gods split the ancient earth goddess Coatlicue in two (in another myth, mother of Huitzilopochtli) in order to create the world from her body parts (for an elaborate interpretation of the whole event see Bonifaz Nuño 1986). The opposition Quetzalcóatl/Tezcatlipoca is sometimes perceived as one of the fundamental oppositions of ancient Mesoamerica. A single lord of duality, Ometeotl, is considered by Carrasco to be "the fundamental divine power in central Mesoamerican religion" (in Hinnels 1984: 241). Dual creator gods that also stand for the opposite forces of nature (light/darkness; earth/sky) are known from a variety of religious traditions and in the Valley of Mexico this principle of duality (or insistence on binary oppositions) is especially strengthened by the fact that there was a dual shrine on the top of the Aztec Templo Mayor dedicated to both the solar (sky) god, Huitzilopochtli and the water (earth) god, Tlaloc.

It is not clear whether this constitutes actual proof of the importance of dualism in Pre-Columbian Mesoamerica or whether the researchers apply their own distinctions (since from early childhood we are taught to think and perceive clear-cut and distinctive categories). In his article on the earth and sky gods of ancient Mexico, Soustelle wrote,

> Tout phénomène humain est singulier. Il n'est donc pas question de déduire des faits mexicains des lois générales applicables à d'autres temps et à d'autres lieux. Mais la succession des événements dans cette partie du monde offre une riche matière à la réflexion de l'ethnologie et même du philosophe, parce qu'elle permet d'étudier comme en laboratoire les actions et réactions réciproques de sociétés qui correspondent à deux modes de vie fondamentaux de l'humanité: celui des nomades chasseurs et collecteurs et celui des cultivateurs sédentaires (Soustelle 1979a: 83).

But the oppositions multiply and it seems unclear, for example, how to interpret the different aspects of Quetzalcóatl (who is both the Morning Star and the Evening Star, but also Merchant God, Wind God, and connected with the Underworld as Yoalli Ehecatl). There are differences even in the interpretations of the well-known myths, such as the one of the slaying of Coyolxauhqui discussed in the previous chapter. However, recalling the phrase "el verdadero dios" ("the true god") recorded in " Textos de los Informantes Indígenas" and quoted at the conclusion of the last chapter, it seems very indicative of the time when these lines were written down, which were already a time of the "true god" and "true religion." The extent to which this concept was influenced by Christianity and the need to "rationalize" the deities and present them in a way that foreigners (Spaniards) could understand them remains open to debate. As Soustelle would point out, understanding Aztec religion was the key to understanding the Aztecs themselves.

---

repetition. Within the broader community (state or society), this smooth functioning is ensured by the "cult." Therefore, the main difference between the two is in the level of generalization; if the ritual is supposed to ensure a good harvest, the cult ensures the functioning of the whole universe. For definitions and models related to Mesoamerica, see Brundage (1985: 4 ff.).

17. Mayan Folklore from Lake Atitlan

James D. Sexton (translated and edited), *Mayan Folktales. Folklore from Lake Atitlán, Guatemala*. New York: Anchor Books, Doubleday, 1992. 262 pp.

In a total of 35 stories, this edited book offers a rare and at the same time fascinating insight into the folklore, customs, and rituals of the Tzutujil Maya community of San José la Laguna, one of the small picturesque towns that surround lake Atitlán in the Guatemalan highlands (altitude 1577 m). Despite some excellent studies in the past (including S. L. Orellana's "Folk Literature of the Tzutujil Maya" published in *Anthropos* 1975: 839-876), Tzutujils were never as popular for research as their highland Maya neighbors, K'iches and Kaqchikels. This was partly due to historical reasons, since the latter two peoples were the most powerful ones at the time of the Spanish conquest of highland Guatemala (around 1541). Another reason might be that the area around the lake has been relatively inaccessible until the 1980s. The decades-long civil war also hindered access to these communities. Nowadays, the area is experiencing booming tourist activity in and around Panajachel (the largest town in the area and tourist hub) while the overall number of Tzutujils is in a sharp decline. They are mostly confined to the small towns of San José la Laguna, San Pedro la Laguna and surrounding hamlets. In contrast, recent decades have seen a notable increase in the K'iche' population.

The stories were collected by several of Sexton's Tzutujil collaborators, although by far the greatest contribution is by his longtime friend and assistant, Ignacio Bizarro Ujpán (a pseudonym, as are all the other native names in the book). It almost seems that the book should have been co-authored, although Sexton does give full credit to his assistant. On the down side, the stories presented are actually translations of the translations. They were originally told in Tzutujil and subsequently presented to the editor in Spanish so that he could make an English translation.

Although the book is based on extensive fieldwork in the area, Sexton's Introduction gives some information that is based on outdated information, or simply inaccurate. For example, it is hard to see how one could support the claim that "the Indian population share a general Mayan heritage" (xii). There is no sense of a general common heritage (or a "pan-Mayan identity") in the highland Maya area, except among a very small number of intellectuals. People tend to identify primarily with their native town rather than their ethnic group. The claim that the Aztecs "might have conquered the highland Maya" (xv) is simply inaccurate, as is the statement that human sacrifice played a relatively minor role in the Mayan highlands (xix).

I also strongly object to Sexton's use of the term "dialect" when referring to Mayan languages (pages xiii and xvi). The distinction between dialect and language is quite important since it has been invoked to justify the repression of native languages and related heritages by governments through Latin American, especially in Guatemala. In this discriminatory terminology native (Amerindian) languages are called (in Spanish) *"idiomas"* (or dialects), not *"lenguas"* (languages). Hence, native languages are reduced (culturally, politically, etc.) to a form of communication employed by lower class people. The main colonial language is *the language* – the rest are mere *dialects*.

The world that one encounters in these stories is filled with shamans, magic, and witchcraft. Numerous myths and legends are told and re-told, including the one on the origin of the world. Among the most intriguing are the ones that display a unique mixture of the native Tzutujil and Christian heritage, such as the story of the Dance of the Deer (58-64). The editor himself points out that "it often is difficult to tell whether a given tale has Old World or New World roots" (xxiii).

Despite some objections, it is my hope that this very general, well-written, and readable book will open up a new horizon for the ethnological, linguistic, and anthropological research in the highland Maya region, the world of the Tzutujil Mayas.

FIG. 11. STRUCTURE 2, IXIMCHE. THE TEMPLE WAS PROBABLY 19 METERS HIGH WHEN IT WAS COMPLETED. IT WAS BUILT AFTER 1470, WHEN KAQCHIQUELS ESTABLISHED THEIR CAPITAL, AND COMPLETED BEFORE 1524.

18. Lacandon Stories

Didier Boremanse, *Contes et mythologie des Indiens lacandons: Contribution à l'étude de la tradition orale maya*. Paris: L'Harmattan, 1986. 407 pp., 11 photos.

Lacandon Maya from the tropical forests of the Mexican state of Chiapas have been regarded as living examples of "survivals." In their case, they were supposed to be the last example of the survival of the "original" spiritual and cultural traditions of the ancient Mesoamerica. However, "True Men" (*hach winik* as they call themselves), once thought to be near extinction, today live in three communities summing some 1,000 people and have become a tourist attraction. They are also important agents in the struggle to stop logging and preserve the forest. This struggle, beginning around 1979 with the help of photographer and long-time ally, Gertrude Blom, may well be the first modern ecological movement. Taking into account the nuances of the acculturative process, they were, nevertheless, considered to embody Rousseau's ideal of the *noble sauvage*. Yet selling "authentic" hand-made souvenirs to tourists does not generate much profit. Scholars, though, are fascinated by the breadth of cultural influences shown in their rituals. These combine "traditional" Mayan beliefs with ones from Mexico's central plateau (from whence they probably migrated to the present-day Mexican state of Chiapas during the 11th and 12th centuries CE), as well as with some parts of the Christian faith, presumably as a result of sporadic contact with the Spanish until 18th century. The very fact that there are Indians who have lived in the jungle ("in the wilderness") for the last five centuries, and who have never formally acknowledged the authority of "official" state institutions (even though they completely depend on the Mexican Government for medication and tools), has attracted ethnologists and anthropologists since the early 20th century. Alfred M. Tozzer did fieldwork during the three year period between 1902 and 1905 and in 1907 published *A Comparative Study of the Mayas and the Lacandons*. Other important texts dealing with religion and myths of the Lacandons were later published by Cline (1944) and Georgette Soustelle (1959), and they proved to be quite influential in anthropological and ethnohistorical research on contemporary Mayan communities. However, the study of Lacandons really takes off during the late 1960s, first with Robert Bruce and later with a young Belgian researcher, Didier Boremanse (b. 1948).

After studying at the Catholic University in Leuven, Boremanse earned his M.A. and Ph.D. in social anthropology at Oxford. He later taught at the Universidad del Valle del Guatemala, where he was also Professor and Head of the Department until 2006. Boremanse has already established himself as an authority on Lacandon myths through an article he published in 1982. However, the present collection of myths and tales is the most complete contribution to Lacandon ethnology and probably one of the most important works for the understanding of contemporary Mayan communities. A German edition was published almost simultaneously with the French, and translations followed in English and Spanish. Didier Boremanse is an extraordinary scholar, with impressive research experience. He is also confident enough to provide opinions of his colleagues that he disagrees with (usually in footnotes) – enabling his readers to compare different points of view and to draw their own conclusions. This book compares favourably with many other volumes dealing with myths and belief systems published in recent decades. Numerous bibliographic references cover all the relevant literature published until 1984 (they have been updated in subsequent editions of the book – in German, Spanish, English, and other languages[26]), and he also made use of some not easily accessible archival materials from Guatemala.

Myths and stories in this book are divided in two sections. The first comprises 50 tales that are part of the "Folklore and Mythology of the Northern Lacandons," while the second includes 42 contributions in the "Stories and Mythology of the Southern Lacandons." Taken together they provide a valuable source for studying oral literature. Boremanse has managed to make them accessible to non-specialists as well and also includes parts of the stories written down by other researchers (like Bruce). This helps place myths and stories in logical and coherent contexts. As a result the wonderful world of these inhabitants of the Chiapas rainforest becomes surprisingly clear and interesting. Having said that, perhaps Boremanse could have done more to address the meaning of the ancient Maya cities like Palenque and Yaxchilán for the Lacandons, especially when referring to the ceremonies they perform in the ruins of these long-abandoned cities. On one level this could be related to the Classic Maya civilization (3rd – 9th centuries CE), but by the time Lacandons arrived in the area (11th century CE at the earliest), ruins were all that was left of that civilization. People interested in pre-Columbian cultures probably would not mind reading some additional notes on the relationship between myths and history, and those who encounter the world of the Maya for the first time would have also found these very helpful. Also, it is a pity that this book went into press almost simultaneously with the publication of McGee's excellent article on the survival of "Classic" Mayan beliefs among the contemporary Lacandons since it would have been interesting to see Boremanse's response the depictions of deities and their functions at odds with his account.

But these are mostly technical quibbles having mostly to do with the style of writing, as well as (with reference to publications being printed almost simultaneously) to things over which the author had no influence. Overall, the present book is like a detailed, but still very compact and readable, miniature encyclopaedia of Lacandon culture, and it will be most useful for scholars and non-specialists in many decades to come.

---

[26] Two of the stories were also translated into Serbo-Croatian by Marijana Strizić and published in the literary journal *Književna reč* No. 341, pp. 6-7, 10 April 1989.

19. A Discourse-Centred Approach to Myths and Culture

Greg Urban, *A Discourse-Centered Approach to Culture: Native South American Myths and Rituals.* Austin: University of Texas Press, 1991. viii+ 215 pp., 13 figures, 1 map, bibliography, index. (Texas Linguistics Series.)

This book combines the results of recent developmenls in critical theory (especially the "post-structuralist" or "deconstructuralist" approach exemplified in the works of the late French philosopher Michel Foucault) and Urban's own ethnographic research among the Shokleng lndians of the southernmost part of the Brazilian Plateau. The "discourse-centered approach to language and culture" that the author advocates developed from discussions with his colleagues at the University of Texas at Austin, especially Joel Scherzer, to whom Urban gives full credit for the title of the book (23). The book contains a wealth of ethnographic data, especially on South American ritual narratives, and focuses on some important theoretical issues. This outline will be concerned primarily with those theoretical issues.

Discourse analysis as outlined by Foucault (*L'Archeologie du savoir*, 1969 – not referred to directly in this book, but with whose concepts Urban is undoubtedly familiar) proposes to look at things in the context when and where they occur. This shift from text to context has been the most profound legacy of the "deconstructuralist" Foucault. The shift also involves sereral distinctive methodological approaches – structuralist, semiotic, hermeneutic – and it is interesting to look at the theoretical questions addressed in the book.

Urban sees culture as "localized in concrete, publicly accessible signs, the most important of which are actually occurring instances of discourse" (1). Culture can be "conceptualized as a collection of history of discourse instances" (p. 18), so it is defined as "a collection or history of publicly accessible sign vehicles, the most important being instances of discourse" (19). Actually, the "sign vehicle" is primarily associated with the semiotic approach of C. S. Pierce. Urban does not define this important concept, and refers to Pierce only indirectly on page 13. "If anthropologists are to understand culture, they need to understand the properties of discourse that make it attractive" (102). Discourse is defined as "the means by which the past is kept alive in the present, by means of which a culture is maintained" (17). However, the author also notes that "to comment upon discourse is also to produce discourse – metadiscourse, which is itself worth of ethnographic description. What individuals say about what they say is not necessarily identical to what they in fact say" (7).

This brings us to the problems of interpretation in the social sciences. In the American academia, the interpretative approach has been promoted since the 1950s by R. Bellah and C. Geertz. In terms of structure, the interpretative approach has been utilized in social anthropology by V. W. Turner, M. Spiro and M. Sahlins, and research concerned with the relationship between writing and ethnography followed later in the works of P. Rabinow, J. Clifford, and G. Marcus.

Urban refers to the work of the Swiss linguist Ferdinand de Saussure (1857-1913) when referring to his own method, which is essentially a semiotic one. The problem with this is that Saussure's structuralism cannot be successfully applied to the data outside linguistics. Saussure was himself primarily concerned with the classification of sciences – not with their overall methodology. Here, and especially when he turns to the analysis of particular myths, Urban turns to Lévi-Strauss and his structuralist approach. The assumption (with which I strongly disagree) is that there is a continuum from the structuralism and semiotics (French *sémiologie*) of Saussure to the structuralism of Lévi-Strauss. Urban takes linguistic discourse as a starting point of his study, observing that "as a semiotic system, language has the unusual property of allowing its users to speak about speech as well as about other types of action" (57).

The application of Lévi-Strauss's concepts has been effectively criticized both in regard to social anthropology (for example, Geertz wrote about the "cerebral savage" [1973]) and the study of myth (by G. S. Kirk [1970]). The extent to which readers will accept Urban's methodology depends to a large extent on whether they accept the concepts associated with the French anthropologist. It should be noted, however, that although Urban claims that he is within the tradition of structuralism, the discourse-centered approach is actually associated with post-structuralism (Foucault). Russian formalism is another strong influence on Urban's approach (the book begins with a quotation from Vladimir Propp).

Urban sees myth as a narrative, a form of (oral) discourse. On the semantic level, it is not always clear how myth is different from other forms of discourse (and it is). Urban presents several examples of brilliant formal analyses (sometimes comparable to the Russian school of the study of myth – E. Meletinski, for example), and his insistence on binary (dyadic) oppositions does effectively put him within the Saussurean tradition. No attempt is made to define ritual, which is seen in the specific context of different life situations (for example, the wailing rituals).

Some of the questions concerning the acquisition of data in ethnographic research place Urban closer to certain aspects of interpretative anthropology. Another tradition in which this kind of work may fit is the semiotic one, as shown by the impressive analysis of the stylistic message in the sixth chapter of the book:

> It is possible to think of the discourse as carrying two messages: one semantic or referential, decodable only through mastery of the language in question, the other indexical and iconic, understandable through ambiguities and similarities that can be apprehended independently of those forming the basis of language. One is directly accessible to consciousness – moreover, forms the content of consciousness, the other [indexical and iconic – A. B.] is only indirectly accessible to consciousness, residing first and foremost in the sensuous and phenomenal realms. (123-124)

Within these limits, Urban has produced a volume of admirable scholarship. This book will probably not be a best-seller due to its strong emphasis on theory. Still, there is enough material devoted to the ethnography of speaking (chapters 2-5) – cases of grammatical parallelism in narratives in different parts of the New World, examination of the role of the quoted speech, study of discourse and context, etc. – to satisfy even the most demanding ethnographers. While the book has been written primarily for students (and scholars) of linguistics, the last three chapters (6, 7, and 8) will be of considerable interest to social anthropologists, especially those concerned with methodological issues and methods derived from literary theory. Particularly intriguing is the seventh chapter, "Style and the Meaning of Emotion," which begins with an analysis of Durkheim's account from the *Elementary Forms of Religious Life* (1912) and proceeds to comparison of South American native traditions. This book also opens a brand new world of possible research with the focus on the structure of expressions (poetical, mythical, etc.).

Bibliography

Adams, Richard E. W. 1971. *The Ceramics of Altar de Sacrificios*. Cambridge, MA: Peabody Museum. (Papers of the Peabody Museum of Archaeology and Ethnology, Harvard University Vol. 63, No. 1.)

Adams, Richard E. W.. 1986. Río Azul. *National Geographic* 169(4): 420-450.

Adams, Richard E. W.. 1989. Personal communication. A letter to the author, dated 14 June 1989.

Adams, Richard E. W.. 1999. *Río Azul: An Ancient Maya City*. Norman: University of Oklahoma Press.

Adams, Richard E. W.. 2005. *Prehistoric Mesoamerica*. Revised edition. Norman: University of Oklahoma Press.

Adams, Richard E. W. (ed.) 1987. *Río Azul Reports Number 3, the 1985 Season*. San Antonio: University of Texas at San Antonio.

Alexander, Hartley Burr. 1920. *Latin American Mythology*. Boston: Marshall Jones Co. (Mythology of all Races, 11.)

Anawalt, Patricia R. 1982. Understanding Aztec Human Sacrifice. *Archaeology* 35(5): 38-45.

Andres, Ferdinand. 1963. *Das Pantheon der Maya*. Graz: Akademische Druck und Verlagsanstalt.

Anders, Ferdinand, Maarten Jansen, and Luis Reyes Garcia. 1991. *El libro del Ciuacoatl: Homenaje para el año del Fuego Nuevo. Libro explicativo del Ilamado Códice Borbónico*. Commentary by Ferdinand Anders, Maarten Jansen, and Luis Reyes García. With reproduction of the 1974 edition. Graz: Akademische Druck- u. Verlagsanstalt; Madrid: Sociedad Estatal Quinto Centenario; México: Fondo de Cultura Económica.

Barrera Vásquez, Alfredo, y Sylvia Rendón. 1948. *El Libro de los Libros de Chilam Balam. Traducción de sus textos paralelos*. México: Fondo de Cultura Económica.

Barton Robertson, Martha. 1991. *Mexican Manuscript Painting: A Catalog of the Latin American Library Collection*. New Orleans: Tulane University.

Baudez, Claude-François. 1984. Le roi, la balle et le maïs. Images du jeu du balle maya. *Journal de la Société des Américanistes* 70(1): 139-151.

Baudez, Claude-François. 2002. *Une histoire de la religion des Mayas. Du panthéisme au pantheon*. Paris: Albin Michel.

Baudez, Claude-François. 2004. *Les Mayas*. Paris: Belles Lettres.

Baudez, Claude François, et Pierre Becquelin. 1984. *Les Mayas*. Paris: Gallimard.

Baudez, Claude-François, et Sydney Picasso. 1987. *Les cités perdues des Mayas*. Paris: Gallimard.

Bernal, Ignacio. 1962. *Bibliografía de arqueología y etnografía. Mesoamérica y Norte de México, 1514-1960*. México: Instituto Nacional de Antropología e Historia. (Memorias, 7)

Beyer, Hermann. 1928. Symbolic Ciphers in the Eyes of the Maya Deities. *Anthropos* 23: 32-37.

Bonifaz Nuño, Rubén. 1986. *Imágen de Tlaloc: Hipótesis iconográfica y textual*. México: UNAM.

Boremanse, Didier. 1982. A comparative study in Lacandon Maya mythology. *Journal de la Société des Américanistes* 68(1): 71-98.

Bošković, Aleksandar. 1986a. Quetzalcoatl - Kukulcan - Paleuleukang. *Polja* 327: 248-250.

Bošković, Aleksandar.. 1986b. Značenje majanskih mitova [The Meaning of Maya Myths]. *Polja* 334: 520-524.

Bošković, Aleksandar.. 1988a. Kecalkoatl/"Pernata Zmija" [Qutzalcóatl/"Feathered Serpent"]. *Knjiĭževna reč* 330: 13.

Bošković, Aleksandar.. 1988b. Mit o rodjenju Uinala. [Myth of the birth of the Uinal.] *Bulletin of the Ethnographic Institute of the SASA* Vol. 36-37, pp. 131-138.

Bošković, Aleksandar.. 1989a. Usmena književnost Maja. [Oral literature of the Mayas.] *Knjiĭževna reč* 341: 6.

Bošković, Aleksandar.. 1989b. Na tragu potomaka jaguara. [On the trail of the Jaguar's children]. In: A. Bošković (ed.) 1989; pp. 65-72.

Bošković, Aleksandar.. 1989c. Religije prošlosti, drugi put. [Religions of the past, second time.] *Polja* 360: 62-63.

Bošković, Aleksandar.. 1990. *Religija i kultura Maja. [Maya Religion and Culture.]* Belgrade: Opus.

Bošković, Aleksandar.. 2002. Anthropological Perspectives on Myth. *Anuário Antropológico* 99: 103-144.

Bošković, Aleksandar.. 2006. *Mit politika ideologija. Ogledi iz komparativne antropologije. [Myth, Politics, Ideology: Essays in Comparative Anthropology.]* Belgrade: Institute of Social Sciences.

Bošković, Aleksandar (ed.) 1989. *Religija i umetnost Olmeka.* [Olmec Religion and Art.] Special issue of the journal *Vidici* nos. 261/262, pp. 5-73. With contributions by Beatriz de la Fuente, David C. Grove, and Ulrich Köhler. Belgrade.

Bošković, Aleksandar, Milan Vukomanović, and Zoran Jovanović. (eds.) 2015. *Rečnik božanstava i mitskih ličnosti sveta. [Dictionary of World Deities and Mythic Persons.]* Belgrade: Službeni glasnik and Institute of Social Sciences.

Bricker, Victoria R. 1983. Directional Glyphs in Maya Inscriptions and Codices. *American Antiquity* 48(2): 347-353.

Brodie, Neal, and Colin Renfrew. 2005. Looting and the World's Archaeological Heritage: The Inadequate Response. *Annual Review of Anthropology* 34: 343-361.

Brown, Betty Ann. 1977. *European Influences in Early Colonial Descriptions and Illustrations of the Mexica Monthly Calendar.* PhD Dissertation. Albuquerque: Department of Art History, University of New Mexico.

Brown, Betty Ann. 1979. Deities of the Codex Borbonicus. Paper read at the 43rd International Congress of Americanists, Vancouver.

Brundage, Burr Cartwright. 1979. *The Fifth Sun: Aztec Gods, Aztec World.* Austin: University of Texas Press.

Brundage, Burr Cartwright. 1985. *The Jade Steps: A Ritual Life of the Aztecs.* Salt Lake City: University of Utah Press.

Carrasco, Davíd. 1987a. Aztec Religion. In: Mircea Eliade (gen ed.), *Encyclopedia of Religion* 2: 23-29. New York: Macmillan.

Carrasco, Davíd. 1987b. Coatlicue. In: Mircea Eliade (gen ed.), *Encyclopedia of Religion* 3: 551. New York: Macmillan.

Carrasco, Davíd. 1987c. Human Sacrifice: Aztec Rites. In: Mircea Eliade (gen ed.), *Encyclopedia of Religion* 6: 518-523. New York: Macmillan.

Caso, Alfonso. 1953. Un problema de interpretación. *Yan* 2: 105-107.

Caso, Alfonso. 1967. *Calendarios prehispánicos.* México: Instituto de Investigaciones Históricas, UNAM.

Clendinnen, Inga. 1987. *Ambivalent Conquests: Maya and Spaniards in Yucatan, 1517-1570.* Cambridge: Cambridge University Press.

Cline, Howard. 1944. Lore and Deities of the Lacandon Indians, Chiapas, Mexico. *Journal of American Folklore* 57(224): 107-115.

Codex Borbonicus. 1899. *Codex Borbonicus. Manuscrit Mexicain de la Bibliotheque du Palais Bourbon.* Published in facsimile with the commentary, M. E.-T. Hamy. Paris: Ernest Leroux.

Codex Borbonicus. 1938. *Códice Borbonico.* Manuscrito pictórico antiguo Mexicano que se conserva en la Biblioteca de la Cámara de Diputados de Paris. (Palais Bourbon.) Edition of 25 copies. México: Libreria anticuaria G. M. Echaniz.

Codex Borbonicus. 1940. *A Sacred Almanac of the Aztecs.* (Tonalamatl of the Codex Borbonicus.) Edited by George C. Vaillant. [no data about the publisher]

Codex Borbonicus. 1974. *Codex Borbonicus. Bibliothéque de L'Assemblée Nationale – Paris (Y 120).* Facsimile of the Codex in the original format, with commentaries by Karl Anton Nowotny and Jacqueline de Durand-Forest. Graz: Akademische Druck-u. Verlagsanstalt.

Coe, Michael D. 1989. The Royal Fifth. Earliest Notices of Maya writing. Washington: Center for Maya Research. (Research Reports on Maya Writing, 28.)

Coe, Michael D. 2000. *Breaking the Maya Code.* Revised ed. Harmondsworth: Penguin.

Coe, Michael D. 2011. *The Maya.* 8th edition. London: Thames and Hudson.

Coe, Michael D., Dean R. Snow, and Elizabeth P. Benson. 1986. *Atlas of Ancient America.* New York: Facts on File.

Coe, William R. 1965. Tikal, Guatemala, and Emergent Maya Civilization. *Science* Vol. 147, No. 3664, pp. 1401-1419.

Coe, William R. 1988. *Tikal: A Handbook of the Ancient Maya Ruins.* 2nd ed. With revisions by Carlos Rudy Larios V. Philadelphia: University of Pennsylvania Press.

Coe, William R. 1990. *Excavations in the Great Plaza, North Terrace, and North Acropolis of Tikal. Tikal Report No. 14.* 6 Vols. Philadelphia: University of Pennsylvania Museum. (Museum Monographs, 61.)

Coggins, Clemency 1985. Maya Iconography. In: Charles Gallenkamp and Regina Elise Johnson (eds.), *Maya: Treasures of an Ancient Civilization,* pp. 47-57. New York: The Albuquerque Museum, in association with Harry N. Abrams, Inc.

Couch, N. C. Christopher. 1985. *The Festival Cycle of the Aztec Codex Borbonicus.* Oxford: BAR. (BAR International Series, 270.)

Courlander, Harold. (ed.) 1982. *Hopi Voices: Recollections, Traditions, and Narratives of the Hopi Indians.* Albuquerque: University of New Mexico Press.

Davies, Nigel. 1982. *The Ancient Kingdoms of Mexico.* Harmondsworth: Penguin.

Debeljak, Anton 1937. Azteška omika. [The Aztec Culture]. *Življenje in svet* 11/3. [no data on the pages available]

Del Paso y Troncoso, Francisco. 1979. [1898.] *Descripción, historia y exposición del Códice Borbónico.* México: Siglo Veintiuno.

Demarest, Arthur A. 2004. *Ancient Maya: The Rise and Fall of a Rainforest Civilization.* Cambridge: Cambridge University Press.

Demarest, Arthur A. 2013. The Collapse of the Classic Maya Kingdoms of the Southwestern Petén: Implications for the End of Classic Maya Civilization. In *Millenary Maya Societies: Past Crises and Resilience,* edited by M.-Charlotte Arnauld and Alain Breton, pp. 22-48. Electronic document, published online at Mesoweb: www.mesoweb.com/ publications/MMS/2_Demarest.pdf.

Dibble, Charles E. 1980. The Xalaquia Ceremony. *Estudios de Cultura Náhuatl* 14: 197-202.

Duran, Diego. 1867. [1581.] *Historia de las Indias de Nueva España e islas de Tierra Firme*. 2 t. México: Imprenta de J. M. Andrade y F. Escalante.

Durkheim, Émile. 1912. *Les formes élémentaires de la vie religieuse. Le système totémique en Australie*. Paris: PUF.

Dütting, Dieter. 1976. The Great Goddess in Classic Maya Religious Belief. *Zeitschrift für Ethnologie* 101: 41-146.

Duverger, Christian. 1991. Jacques Soustelle 1912-1990. In: *Encyclopaedia Universalis*, pp. 625-626. Paris.

Edmonson, Munro S. 1960. Nativism, Syncretism, and Anthropological Science. In: Munro S. Edmonson (ed.), *Nativism and Syncretism*, pp. 181-204. New Orleans: Middle American Research Institute, Tulane University.

Edmonson, Munro S. 1964. Historia de las Tierras altas mayas, según los documentos indígenas. In: Alberto Ruz (ed.), *Desarrrollo cultural de los mayas*, pp. 255-278. México: UNAM.

Edmonson, Munro S. (ed. and translated) 1971. *The Book of Counsel: The Popol Vuh of the Quiché Maya of Guatemala*. New Orleans: Middle American Research Institute, Tulane University.

Edmonson, Munro S. 1978. Los Popol Vuh. *Estudios de Cultura Maya* 11: 249-266.

Edmonson, Munro S. 1979. Some Postclassic Questions about the Classic Maya. *Estudios de Cultura Maya* 12: 157-166.

Edmonson, Munro S. (ed. and translated.) 1986. *Heaven Born Merida and its Destiny: The Book of the Chilam Balam of Chumayel*. Austin: University of Texas Press.

Estrada-Belli, Francisco. 2006. Lightning Sky, Rain, and the Maize God: The Ideology of Preclassic Maya Rulers at Cival, Peten, Guatemala. *Ancient Mesoamerica* 17(1): 57-78.

Farris, Nancy M. 1984. *Maya Society under Colonial Rule: The Collective Enterprise of Survival*. Princeton: Princeton University Press.

Fernández, Justino. 1963. Aproximación a Coyolxauhqui. *Estudios de Cultura Náhuatl* 4: 37-54.

Foncerrada de Molina, Marta, y Sonia Lombardo de Ruiz. 1979. *Vasijas pintadas mayas en contexto arqueológico. (Catálogo)*. México: UNAM.

Foucault, Michel. 1969. *L'Archéologie du savoir*. Paris: Gallimard.

Fuente, Beatriz de la. 1972. La escultura olmeca como expression religiosa. In: Jaime Litvak King y Noemi Castillo Tejero (eds.), *Religión en Mesoamérica: XII mesa redonda*, pp. 79-84. México: Sociedad Mexicana de Antropología.

Gann, Thomas W. F. 1918. *The Maya Indians of Southern Yucatan and Northern British Honduras*. Washington: Government Printing Office. (Bulletin of the Bureau of American Ethnology, 64.)

Garibay, Fray Ángel Ma. K. 1971. *Historia de la literatura náhuatl*. 2ª ed., pról. de Miguel León-Portilla. México: Editorial Porrua. (Collección "Sepan Cuantos...", 662.)

Garza Camino, Mercedes de la. 2007. Palenque como *imago mundi* y presencia en ella de Itzamná. *Estudios de Cultura Maya* 30: 15-36.

Garza Camino, Mercedes de la, y Martha Ilia Nájera Coronado. (eds.) 2002. *Religión maya*. Madrid: Editorial Trotta. (Enciclopedia Iberoamericana de Religiones, 2.)

Geertz, Clifford. 1973. *The Interpretation of Cultures*. New York: Basic Books.

Geertz, Clifford. 1988. *Works and Lives: An Anthropologist as Author*. Stanford: Stanford University Press.

Glass, John B. 1975. A Survey of Native Middle American Pictorial Manuscripts. In: *Handbook of Middle American Indians* 14: 3-80. Austin: University of Texas Press.

Glass, John B., and Donald Robertson. 1975. A Census of Native Middle American Pictorial Manuscripts. In: *Handbook of Middle American Indians* 14: 81-252. Austin: University of Texas Press.

González Torres, Yolotl. 1991. *Diccionario de mitología y religión de Mesoamérica*. México: Larousse.

Graham, Ian. 2002. Review of Colin Renfrew, *Loot, Legitimacy and Ownership: The Ethical Crisis in Archaeology*. *Antiquity* 76: 908-909.

Grove, David C. 1973. Olmec Altars and Myths. *Archaeology* 26(2): 128-135.

Grove, David C. 1999. Public Monuments and Sacred Mountains: Observations on Three Formative Period Sacred Landscapes. In: David Grove and Rosemary Joyce (eds.), *Social Patterns in Pre-Classic Mesoamerica*, pp. 255-299. Washington (DC): Dumbarton Oaks Research Library and Collection.

Grove, David C. 2014. *Discovering the Olmecs: An Unconventional History*. Austin: University of Texas Press.

Grube, Nikolai, and Maria Gaida. 2006. *Die Maya. Schrift und Kunst*. Köln: SMB-Du Mont.

Gunsenheimer, Antje. 2002. *Geschichtstradierung in den yukatekischen Chilam Balam-Büchern: Eine Analyse der Herkunft und Entwicklung ausgewählter historischer Berichte*. PhD Dissertation, Faculty of Philosophy, University of Bonn.

Gutierrez, Carlos. 1878. *Fray Bartolomé de Las Casas: sus tiempos y su apostolado*. Madrid: Imp. de Fortanet.

Hanke, Lewis, and A. Millares Carlo (eds.) 1943. *Cuerpo de documentos del siglo XVI sobre los derechos de España en las Indias y las Filipinas*. México: Fondo de Cultura Económica.

Hinnels, John R. (ed.) 1984. *Dictionary of Religions*. Harmondsworth: Penguin.

Holmquist Pachas, Ulla, y Javier Bellina de los Heros. 2010. *Historia del Perú II. El Perú Antiguo II (200 a. C. - 500) El período de los desarrollos regionales*. Lima: Empresa Editora El Comercio S.A.

Houston, Stephen, and David Stuart. 1989. The *Way* Glyph: Evidence for "Co-essences" among the Classic Maya. *Research Reports on Ancient Maya Writing*, 30. Washington, DC: Center for Maya Research.

Houston, Stephen, and David Stuart. 1996. Of Gods, Glyphs and Kings: Divinity and Rulership Among the Classic Maya. *Antiquity* 70: 289-312.

Hultkrantz, Åke. 1979. *The Religions of the American Indians*. Translated by Monica Setterwall. Berkeley and Los Angeles: University of California Press.

Hvidtfeldt, Arild. 1958. *Teotl and *Ixiptlatli. Some Central Conceptions in Ancient Mexican Religion with a General Introduction on Cult and Myth*. Copenhagen: Munksgaard.

Izquierdo-Egea, Pascual. 2015. El colapso del clásico tardío entre los mayas de Uaxactún (Guatemala) y Barton Ramie (Belice) según el registro funerario. *Arqeología Iberoamericana* 27: 12-32.

Jambrušić, A. 1885. Bartolomej de las Casas i borba za slobodu Indijanaca [Bartolomé de Las Casas and the Indians' struggle for freedom]. *Katolički list* 36: 41-44.

Jansen, Maarten, and Gabina Aurora Pérez Jiménez. 2004. Renaming the Mexican Codices. *Ancient Mesoamerica* 15: 267-271.

Jiménez Moreno, Wigberto. 1941. Tula y los toltecas según las fuentes históricas. *Revista Mexicana de Estudios Antropológicos* 5: 39-43.

Jiménez Moreno, Wigberto. 1971. ¿Religión o religiones mesoamericanas? Symposium Religiones Mesoamericanas (1. Religión prehispánica), organizado por Alfonso Caso. *Verhandlungen des XXXVIII. Internationalen Amerikansitenkongresses, Stuttgart-München 12. bis 18. August 1968*, Vol. 3, pp. 201-206. Munich: Renner.

Jones, Grant D. 1989. *Maya Resistance to Spanish Rule*. Albuquerque: University of New Mexico Press.

Jones, Grant D. 1998. *The Conquest of the Last Maya Kingdom*. Stanford: Stanford University Press.

Kampen, M. E. 1981. The Religion of the Maya. *Iconography of Religions* XI/4. Leiden: E. J. Brill.

Kirk, G. S. 1970. *Myth: Its Meaning and Functions in Ancient and Other Cultures*. Cambridge: Cambridge University Press.

Köhler, Ulrich. 1985. Olmeken und Jaguare: Zur Deutung von Mischwesen des präklassisches Kunst Mesoamerikas. *Anthropos* 80(1): 15-52.

Knorozov, Jurij V. 1964. Pantheon of Ancient Maya. *Proceedings of the Seventh International Congress of Anthropological and Ethnological Sciences*. Moscow: Nauka. [offprint]

Kubler, George. 1972. La evidencia intrínseca y la analogía etnológica en el estudio de las religiones mesoamericanas. In. Jaime Litvak King y Noemi Castillo Tejero (eds.), *Religión en Mesoamérica: XII Mesa redonda*, pp. 1-24. México: Sociedad Mexicana de Antropología.

Kubler, George. 1984. An Aztec Calendar of 20,176 Non-Repeating Years in *Codex Borbonicus*, pp. 21-22. *Indiana* 9: 123-136.

Kubler, George. 1990. *Art and Architecture of Ancient America*. 4th revised ed. Harmondsworth: Pelican.

Landa, Diego de. 1985. [1566.] *Relación de las cosas de Yucatán*. Edición Miguel Rivera Dorado. Madrid: História 16.

Las Casas, Bartolomé de. 1909. *Apologética Historia de las Indias*. Vol. I. Madrid: Bailly, Bailliére e Hijos.

Las Casas, Bartolomé de. 2006. [1552.] *Brevísima relación de la destruición de las Indias*. Edición André Saint Lu. 14ª edición. Madrid: Catedra.

Lazarević, Aleksandra-Sanja. 1977. *Život i djelo braće Seljan*. [*The Life and Work of the Seljan Brothers*]. Zagreb: Ethnographic Museum.

León-Portilla, Miguel. 1959. *Visión de los vencidos: Relaciones indígenas de la conquista*. México: UNAM.

León-Portilla, Miguel. 1961. *Los antiguos Mexicanos a través de sus crónicas y cantares*. México: Fondo de Cultura Económica.

León-Portilla, Miguel. 1963. Mito del nacimiento de Huitzilopochtli. [Translation; in:] Justino Fernández: Aproximación a Coyolxauhqui, *Estudios de Cultura Náhuatl* 4: 37-54.

León-Portilla, Miguel. 1971. *De Teotihuacán a los Aztecas: Fuentes e interpretaciones históricas*. México: UNAM.

León-Portilla, Miguel. 1979. *Drevni Meksikanci u hronikama i pesmama*. Translated by Branislav Prelević. Sarajevo: Svjetlost; Novi Sad: Matica Srpska; Beograd: Prosveta. [Serbo-Croatian translation of León-Portilla 1961.]

León-Portilla, Miguel. 1980a. *Toltecayotl. Aspectos de la cultura Náhuatl*. México: Fondo de Cultura Económica.

León-Portilla, Miguel. (ed.) 1980b. *Native American Spirituality*. New York: Paulist Press.

León-Portilla, Miguel. 1987. Mesoamerican Religions: Pre-Columbian Religions. In: Mircea Eliade (gen ed.), *Encyclopedia of Religion* 9: 392-406. New York: Macmillan.

León-Portilla, Miguel. 1999. Ometeotl, el supremo Dios dual, y Tezcatlipoca "Dios principal." *Estudios de Cultura Náhuatl* 30: 133-152.

Lessa, William A., and Evon Z. Vogt. (eds.) 1979. *Reader in Comparative Religion: An Anthropological Approach.* 4th edition. New York: Harper & Row.

Lizardi Ramos, César. 1953. Los acompañados del Xiuhmolpilli en el Códice Borbónico. *Yan* 2: 95-101.

López Austin, Alfredo. 1980. *Cuerpo humano y ideología. Las concepciones de los antiguos nahuas.* Tomo I. México: UNAM.

Magni, Caterina. 2003. *Les Olmèques. Des origins au mythe.* Paris: Seuil.

Marcus, Joyce. 2000. Cinco mitos sobre la guerra maya. En: S. Trejo (org.), *La guerra entre los antiguos mayas: memoria de la Primera Mesa Redonda de Palenque*, pp. 225-247. México: INAH y Consejo Nacional para la Cultura y las Artes.

Martínez González, Roberto. 2007. Las entidades anímicas en el pensamiento maya. *Estudios de Cultura Maya* 30: 153-174.

Matos Moctezuma, Eduardo, y Felipe Ehrenberg. 1979. *Coyolxauhqui.* México: Secretaría de Educación Pública.

Meggers, Betty J., Clifford Evans and Emilio Estrada. 1965. Early Formative Period of Coastal Ecuador: The Valdivia and Machalilla Phases. *Smithsonian Contributions to Anthropology*, Volume 1. Washington: Smithsonian Institution Press.

Meza, Otília. 1981. *El Mundo mágico de los dioses del Anáhuac.* México: Editorial Universo México.

McGee, R. John. 1984. The Influence of Prehispanic Maya Religion in Contemporary Lacandon Ritual. *Journal of Latin American Lore* 10(2): 175-187.

McGee, R. John. 1990. *Life, Ritual, and Religion among the Lacandon Maya.* Belmont, CA: Wadsworth.

Momčilović, Vladimir. 1988. Religije prošlosti. [Religions of the past]. *Polja* 358: 548-549.

Montolíu, María. 1980. Los dioses de los cuatro sectores cósmicos y su vínculo con la salud y enfermedad en Yucatán. *Anales de Antropología* XVII, II: 47-65.

Nicholson, Henry B. 1971. The Religion in Pre-Hispanic Central Mexico. In: Gordon F. Ekholm and Ignacio Bernal (eds.), *Archaeology of Northern Mesoamerica*, Part One; *Handbook of Middle American Indians*, pp. 395-446. Austin: University of Texas Press.

Nicholson, Henry B. 1974. Some Remarks on the Provenance of the Codex Borbonicus. *ADEVA Mitteilungen* 40: 14-18.

Nicholson, Henry B. 1976. Preclassic Mesoamerican Iconography from the Perspective of the Post-Classic: Problems in Interpretational Analysis. In: Henry Nicholson (ed.), *Origins of Religious Art Iconography in Preclassic Mesoamerica*, pp. 157-175. Los Angeles: UCLA and Ethnic Arts Council. (UCLA Latin American Studies series 31.)

Nöth, Winfried. 1990. *A Handbook of Semiotics.* Bloomington and Indianapolis: Indiana University Press. (Advances in Semiotics.)

Olivier, Guilhelm, and Roberto Martínez. 2015. Translating Gods: Tohil and Curicaueri in Mesoamerican polytheism in the *Popol Vuh* and the *Relación de Michoacán*. *Ancient Mesoamerica* 26(2): 347-369.

Panofsky, Erwin. 1955. Iconography and Iconology: An Introduction to the Study of Renaissance Art. In: *Meaning in the Visual Arts*, pp. 29-54. Chicago: University of Chicago Press.

Peck, Douglas T. 2005. Re-Examination of Spanish Colonial Period Documents Related to Prehistoric Maya History and Mythology. *Revista de Historia de América* 136: 21-35.

Perera, Victor, and Robert D. Bruce. 1982. *The Last Lords of Palenque: The Lacandon Mayas of the Mexican Rain Forest.* Berkeley: University of California Press.

Poupard, Paul. (sous le dir.) 1993. *Dictionnaire des religions.* 2 Vols. Paris: Presses Universitaires de France.

Quigler, Jeffrey. 2002. Moche politics, religion, and warfare. *Journal of World Prehistory* 16(2): 145-195.

Quiñones Keber, Eloise. 1987. Ritual and Representation in the Tonalamatl of the Codex Borbonicus. *Latin American Indian Literatures Journal* 3(2): 184-195.

Quiñones Keber, Eloise. 1988. The Annual Ritual Cycle in Mesoamerican Manuscripts. *Latin American Indian Literatures Journal* 4(2): 207-225.

Quiñones Keber, Eloise. 2006. Borbonicus, Codex. In: Davíd Carrasco (gen. ed.), *The Oxford Encyclopedia of Mesoamerican Cultures.* http://www.oxfordreference.com/view/10.1093/acref/9780195108156.001.0001/acref-9780195108156-e-53?rskey=GWJgPv&result=53 (Accessed 8 August 2016).

Recinos, Adrian. (ed. and translated) 1947. *Popol Vuh.* México: Fondo de Cultura Económica.

Renfrew, Colin. 2000. *Loot, Legitimacy and Ownership: The Ethical Crisis in Archaeology.* London: Duckworth.

Riese, Berthold. 2011. *Die Maya. Geschichte - Kultur - Religion.* 7. durchgesene Auflage. München: C. H. Beck.

Ristanović, Ljubomir (ed.) 1983a. *Popol Vuh.* Kruševac: Bagdala.

Ristanović, Ljubomir (ed.) 1983b. *Ćilam Balam, knjiga o knjigama.* Kruševac: Bagdala.

Ristanović, Ljubomir (ed.) 1984. *Rodoslov poglavara Totonikapana.* Kruševac: Bagdala.

Rivera Dorado, Miguel. 1981. El rito de la sangre en una terracota maya. *Revista Española de Antropología Americana* 11: 59-67.

Rivera Dorado, Miguel. 1986. *La religión maya.* Madrid: Alianza Editorial.

Rivera Dorado, Miguel. 1991. La religion maya en un solo lugar. *Revista Española de Antropología Americana* 21: 53-76.

Rivera Dorado, Miguel. 2000. Influencia del cristianismo en el Popol Vuh. *Revista Española de Antropología Americana* 30: 137-162.

Robertson, Donald. 1959. *Mexican Manuscript Painting of the Early Colonial Period: The Metropolitan Schools.* New Haven: Yale University Press.

Robertson, William. 1777. *The History of America.* 3 Vols. Dublin: Whitestone, W. Watson, et. al.

Roys, Ralph L. (ed.) 1965. *Ritual of the Bacabs.* Norman: University of Oklahoma Press.

Ruppert, Karl, J. Eric S. Thompson, and Tatiana Proskouriakoff. 1955. *Bonampak, Chiapas, Mexico.* Washington: Carnegie Institution. (Carnegie Institution of Washington Publication 602.)

Sabloff, Jeremy A. 2005. It Depends How We Look at Things: New Perspectives on the Postclassic Period in the Northern Maya Lowlands. *Proceedings of the American Philosophical Society* 151(1): 11-26.

Sabloff, Jeremy A. (ed.) 2003. *Tikal: Dynasties, Foreigners, and Affairs of State.* Santa Fe: School of American Research Press.

Sahagún, Bernardino de. 1999. [ca. 1577.] *Historia General de las cosas de la Nueva España.* 12 t. México: Editorial Porrua. ("Colección sepan cuantos...".)

Saturno, William A., David Stuart, and Boris Beltrán. 2006. Early Maya Writing at San Bartolo, Guatemala. *Science* Vol. 311, No. 5765, pp. 1281-1283.

Seljan, Stevo. N.d. Kurioziteti Centralne Amerike [Curiosities of Central America]. Manuscript in the Archive of the Ethnographic Museum in Zagreb, signed "Stevo", among the manuscripts of the South America under No. 5050/I-B.

Schellhas, Paul. 1904. *Representations of Deities of the Maya Manuscripts*. Translated by Miss Selma Wesselhoeft and Miss A. M. Parker. Cambridge, MA: Peabody Musueum. (Papers of the Peabody Museum of Archaeology and Ethnology, Harvard University Vol. 4, No. 1.)

Scholes, France V., and Ralph Roys. 1948. *The Maya Chontal Indians of Acalan-Tixchel*. Washington: Carnegie Institution. (Carnegie Institution of Washington Publication 560.)

Seler, Eduard. 1902-1923. *Gesammelte Abhandlungen zur Amerikanischen Sprach- und Alterthumskunde*. 5 vols. Berlin: A. Asher.

Sharer, Robert J., and Loa P. Traxler. 2006. *The Ancient Maya*. 6th revised edition. Stanford: Stanford University Press.

Skidmore, Joel. 2005. The Rulers of Palenque. With illustrations by Merle Green Robertson. Mesoweb. http://www.mesoweb.com/palenque/resources/rulers/PalenqueRulers-05.pdf (Accessed 29 August 2016.)

Soustelle, Georgette. 1959. Observations sur la religion des *Lacandons* du Mexique méridional. *Journal de la Société des Américanistes* XLVIII: 141-196.

Soustelle, Jacques. 1940. *La pénsee cosmologique des anciens Mexicains. Représentations de monde et de l'espace*. Paris: Hermann & Cᶦᵉ.

Soustelle, Jacques. 1955. *La vie quotidienne des Aztèques à la veille de la conquête espagnole*. Paris: Hachette.

Soustelle, Jacques. 1967. *Les quatre soleils: Souvenirs et réflexions d'un ethnologue au Mexique*. Paris: Plon.

Soustelle, Jacques. 1979a. *Les Olmèques: la plus ancienne civilisation du Mexique*. Paris: Arthaud.

Soustelle, Jacques. 1979b. *L'universe des Aztèques*. Paris: Hermann.

Stuart, David. 2004. New Year Record in Classic Maya Inscriptions. *PARI Journal* 5(2): 1-6.

Šanjek, Franjo. 1978. *Korčulanin Vinko Paletin, istraživač Yucatana i teoretičar španjolske "conquiste" u XVI. stoljeću. [Vinko Paletin from Korčula, explorer of Yucatan and a theorist of the Spanish "conquista" in the 16th century]*. Croatica Christiana periódica (Zagreb) 2(2): 83-130.

Šanjek, Franjo. 1991. Hrvati otkrivaju ljudska prava. [Croats discover human rights]. *Vjesnik* (Zagreb) 19 January 1991.

Šprajc, Ivan. 2001. *Orientaciones astronómicas en la arquitectura prehispánica del centro de México*. México: INAH.

Šprajc, Ivan. 2009. *Izgubljena mesta. Arheološka iskanja v deželi Majev. [Lost Cities: Archaeological Quests in the Land of the Maya.]* Ljubljana: Založba Modrijan.

Taladoire, Éric. 2003. *Les Mayas*. Paris: Éditions du Chêne.

Taube, Karl. 1992. *The Major Gods of Ancient Yucatan*. Washington: Dumbarton Oaks Research Library and Collection.

Taube, Karl. 1993. *Aztec and Maya Myths*. Austin: University of Texas Press.

Taube, Karl. 2005. The Symbolism of Jade in Classic Maya Religion. *Ancient Mesoamerica* 16(1): 23-50.

Thompson, J. Eric. S. 1933. *Mexico Before Cortez: An Account of the Daily Life, Religion, and Ritual of the Aztec and Kindred Peoples.* New York: Charles Scribner's Sons.

Thompson, J. Eric. S. 1939. Moon Goddess in Middle America with Notes on Related Deities. *Carnegie Institution of Washington Publication* 509: 121-173.

Thompson, J. Eric. S. 1950. *Maya Hieroglyphic Writing: Introduction.* Washington: Carnegie Institution of Washington. (Carnegie Institution of Washington, Publication 589.)

Thompson, J. Eric. S. 1961. A Blood-Drawing Ceremony Painted on a Maya Vase. *Estudios de Cultura Maya* 1: 13-20.

Thompson, J. Eric. S. 1966a. [1954.] *The Rise and Fall of Maya Civilization.* Revised edition. Norman: University of Oklahoma Press.

Thompson, J. Eric. S. 1966b. Merchant Gods in Middle America. In: *Summa anthropologica: en homenaje a Roberto J. Weitlaner*, pp. 159-172. México: INAH.

Thompson, J. Eric. S. 1970. *Maya History and Religion.* Norman: University of Oklahoma Press.

Tomičić, Stjepan. 1935. Propast kraljevstva Maja [Decline of the Maya kingdom]. *Obitelj* 21 [no page numbers available].

Tozzer, Alfred M. 1907. *A Comparative Study of the Mayas and the Lacandones.* New York: Macmillan.

Tozzer, Alfred M. (ed.) 1941. *Landa's Relación de las cosas de Yucatan: A Translation.* Cambridge: Peabody Museum, Harvard University.

Turner, Frederick W., III. 1974. *The Portable North American Indian Reader.* Harmondsworth: Penguin.

Turner, Victor W. 1967. *The Forest of Symbols: Aspects of Ndembu Ritual.* Ithaca (NY): Cornell University Press.

Van Akkeren, Ruud W. 2003. Authors of the Popol Wuj. *Ancient Mesoamerica* 14: 237-256.

Vidal Angles, Carlos, and Marilyn Domínguez Turriza. (eds.) 2003. *Calakmul. Antología.* Campeche: Conaculta/INAH.

Viličić, Melita. 1953. *Predkonkvistadorska Amerika.* [Pre-Conquest America.] Zagreb: Školska knjiga.

Vogt, Evon Z. 1964. Ancient Maya and Contemporary Tzotzil Cosmology: A Comment on Some Methodological Problems. *American Antiquity* 30(2): 192-195.

Vogt, Evon Z. 1969. *Zinacantan: A Maya Community in the Highlands of Chiapas.* Cambridge, MA: Harvard University Press.

Weber, Max. 1946. *From Max Weber: Essays in Sociology.* Translated, edited, and with an Introduction by H. H. Gerth and C. Wright Mills. New York: Oxford University Press.

Wilk, Richard R. 1985. The Ancient Maya and the Political Present. *Journal of Anthropological Research* 41(3): 307-326.

Wisdom, C. 1940. *The Chorti Indians of Guatemala.* Chicago: University of Chicago Press.

Žeravica, Rajko. 1890. *Ruševine u Meksici. [The Ruins in Mexico].* Zastava (Novi Sad) 25: 117.

Glossary

Animal spirit companion

Also *nahual* (from Náhuatl *nahualli* – "occult, hidden, disguise", Spanish *nagual*), the idea present in Postclassic Mesoamerica that all life is interconnected. The moment a human baby is born, a supernatural animal is also born. This animal is the human's *animal spirit companion* and they share the common destiny throughout their lives. Whatever happens to the human, happens to the animal, and vice versa. Spanish conquistadors reported that in Mexico the word referred to a "witch" (Spanish *brujo*), someone with magical powers, who can transform himself into an animal.

Calendar round

A combination of the 260 and 365 days calendar used throughout ancient Mesoamerica. These two cycles, running concurrently, form a cycle of 18,980 days, or 52 years of 365 days. The same date can be repeated in a calendar round, so, for example, the day 1 Reed (when, according to the prophecy, Quetzalcoatl was supposed to come to Mexico) occurred in 1415, 1467, 1519 (the year in which the Spanish conquistadors came), etc.

Chilam Balam

Nine handwritten documents, written in Latin alphabet mostly during the 17th and 18th centuries. The documents are named after Yucatec towns where they originated. They contain a series of historical records, stories and prophecies, as well as some practical information (including recipes), collectively attributed to a *Chilam Balam* or "Jaguar Priest" (Barrera Vásquez y Rendón 1948). Some references in the texts refer to the period during the 16th century and the Spanish conquest (Gunsenheimer 2002). The most famous ones are from Chumayel, Mani and Tizimin (Roys 1967; Edmonson 1982, 1986).

Diffusionism

A methodological approach related to the idea that cultures take elements of other cultures that they come in contact with, propagated especially by German anthropologists at the end of the 19th century. It remained influential among the German-speaking scholars even after the heights of its popularity in the first decades of the 20th century had waned. In contemporary studies it has become popular again with the growing interest in the studies of globalization.

Direct historical approach

A methodological approach according to which observation of contemporary Native American cultures can be used to interpret cultures about which we have insufficient knowledge, most of which predate contemporary ones by more than a 1,000, and sometimes even 3,000 years.

Ethnographic analogy

An approach derived from the *direct historical approach* that uses analogies from present-day communities in order to interpret cultures about which we only have archaeological data, usually without any written evidence. As more archaeological data becomes available, especially with the artefacts (figurines, ceramics, and other types of offerings) found during excavations, the value of this approach has become increasingly questionable.

Intrinsic approach

A methodological approach that emphasises the study of cultures and societies on their own terms, especially in relation to their own system of values. Although historically it can be traced as far back as the ancient Greek philosopher Plato (in his dialogue *Protagoras* from the 5th century BCE), in Mesoamerican studies, it has been emphasised by art historian George Kubler, following on Erwin Panofsky, but also by Mexican historian Wigberto Jiménez Moreno and art historian Beatriz de la Fuente.

Ixiptla

In ancient Mexico, impersonators of the deities that were sacrificed during elaborate ceremonies meant to please these deities. *Ixiptlas* were selected based on their gender and age, in order to correspond to the deities they impersonated as much as possible. During their ritual incarceration (which could last from a couple of weeks to almost a year) they were treated like the gods they represented. Human sacrifice had special meaning in ancient Mesoamerican cultures, since the creation of the world itself was also the result of a sacrifice.

Lords of Day

A group of thirteen deities that preside over different parts of the day. In Postclassic Yucatan they were known as *Oxlahuntiku*, literally "Thirteen who are God."

Lords of Night

A group of nine gods who preside over night. They were also supposed to be in charge of the Underworld. In Postclassic Yucatan, they were known as *Bolontiku*, literally "Nine who are God." Some scholars associate them with death, but they also play important role in rebirth, as can be seen in the *Popol Vuh*.

Mesoamerica

A term coined in 1942 by the German Mexican historian Paul Kirchhoff in order to define the area of high civilizations in Mexico and Central America. Geographically, the area comprised parts of Mexico, the whole of Guatemala and Belize, and parts of Honduras and El Salvador. Mesoamerican societies shared the following characteristics:

1. They were based on the cultivation of corn
2. They all constructed pyramids based on different platforms ("steps")
3. Calendars were of prime importance, both of the 260-day ritual calendar and the 365-day calendar based on the solar year

4. They all had a sacred ball game (which was also played in parts of the present-day US Southwest)
5. They had complex religion and rituals that included human sacrifice
6. All these cultures had hieroglyphic writing
7. Their numerical system was vigesimal (based on the number 20)
8. They all practiced intensive trade and developed highly sophisticated markets.

Náhuatl

Language spoken by the Mexica Aztecs from Central Mexico. It was also the most widely spoken language in Mexico at the time of the Spanish conquest in the 16th century when it served as some sort of a *lingua franca* – similar to Latin in medieval Europe.

New Year ceremony

Among the Mexica Aztecs (14-16th centuries), the celebration of the beginning of the new 52-year cycle (Calendar round) depicted in great detail in the Codex Cihuacoatl (or Codex Borbonicus). The proper ceremonies ensured the well-being of the whole society

Semiotics

Literally, "the science of signs," also referred to by the Swiss linguist Ferdinand de Saussure (when he defined French *sémiologie*) as the "science that studies the life of signs within a society" (quoted in Nöth 1990: 3). Although originally associated with language, in recent decades authors like Umberto Eco strongly emphasised its communicative and cultural component, bringing it closer to anthropology and archaeology. In archaeology, the semiotic approach is usually associated with "post-processual" methodology.

Structuralism

A method of interpretation and analysis of human communication, cognition, and culture, sometimes derived from *semiotics*. In anthropology, its most famous representative was French ethnologist Claude Lévi-Strauss, who around 1940 became acquainted with Saussurean *sémiologie* via the linguist Roman Jakobson and who also was strongly influenced by Russian formalism (as exemplified in Vladimir Propp's *Morphology of the Folktale*).

Tonalamatl

A divinatory almanac used in Central Mexico in the decades before the Spanish conquest.

Tonalpohualli

In Náhuatl, literally "day count," a cycle of 260 days of the Mexica Aztec calendar, each of which is assigned a numerical value from 1 to 13. The 260-day ritual calendar was present throughout Mesoamerica and was especially important for ritual purposes and also for all kind of agricultural activities, harvests, etc.

Trecena

A Spanish word for "thirteen." It refers to the period of 13 days that form a part of *tonalpohualli* in Pre-Columbian Mexico. It corresponds to a week in our calendar.

Yearbearers

In Aztec and Maya calendars, yearbearers or year bearers are one of the four day names of the day on which the 52 year cycle ("century") may begin. In the Central Mexican tradition, they play a special role in the periodic creation and destruction of the world. According to Stuart (2004: 1), only four days could serve as year bearers among the Maya of Postclassic Yucatan: K'an, Muluk, Ix and Kawak. Stuart also claims that they can be found in some Classic Maya texts.

Index